Child Advocacy Within the System

Syracuse Special Education and Rehabilitation Monograph Series, 11

Child Advocacy
Within the System

JAMES L. PAUL,
G. RONALD NEUFELD,
and JOHN W. PELOSI, *Editors*

SYRACUSE UNIVERSITY PRESS   1977

Library of Congress Cataloging in Publication Data
Main entry under title:

Child advocacy within the system.

   (Syracuse special education and rehabilitation monograph series; 11)
   Includes bibliographies and index.
   1.   Children's rights—United States—Addresses, essays, lectures.   2.   Child
welfare—United States—Addresses, essays, lectures.   3.   Children—Institutional
care—United States—Addresses, essays, lectures.   I.   Paul, James L.   II.
Neufeld, G. Ronald.   III.   Pelosi, John W.   IV.   Series: Syracuse University.
Special education and rehabilitation monograph series; 11.
HV741.C47   362.7'0973   76-56365
ISBN 0-8156-0133-6

Foreword

The authors and editors of this book use strong words and phrases in their writing. In these pages the reader will see systems and system-participants referred to as "villains in large institutions" or again as a "nightmare filled with monsters." The situation to which they address themselves is characterized by "despair" and "helplessness," as "impoverished," "corrupting," and one of "mediocrity." "Bureaucratic red tape," they say, results in a "battle of wills," creating a "public school system which houses and nurtures many monsters."

These are angry words of thoughtful men. In my opinion these writers are correct in their observations which gave rise to this book. Children are denied their birthright through the injudicious actions and selfish decisions of bureaucratic system-bound personnel. These people, seemingly secure in the confines of the system, support and protect blatant self-assumed territoriality at the expense of the child, youth, or the adult to whom deserved services are rarely delivered.

With one of the author-editors, we too have urged the consumer to consider the "misfits in the public schools" who fail to provide for the ongoing and developing needs of families whose taxes support the system. While we have long urged the creation of citizen review boards to monitor the administration and the service operations of our social systems, these authors here seek an equally rigorous attack on the problem through advocacy within the system. It must be pointed out that the public school system, a major concern of these authors, is only one system on which they focus their attention. Equally at fault are those who are remiss in their functions within the mental health, social services, and public health systems. Human services delivery and how to improve it is the concern of this book regardless of its title, form, or location: local, state, or national.

While strong words are often used to point up serious problems, the authors of these chapters exploit equally strong words to develop logical arguments to support the employment of a system of advocacy. Is it because of the failure of human beings that advocacy to protect the rights of other human beings is necessary? Do systems themselves create selfishness in the people who operate them? Are all systems so characterized just because they are systems: the schools, the churches, political parties, the many branches of government? Does the presence of a system automatically require the balancing concept of advocacy? We feel that it does.

William M. Cruickshank, Editor
Syracuse Special Education
and Rehabilitation
Monograph Series

Contents

Contributors

William M. Cruickshank is Director of the Institute for Mental Retardation and Related Disabilities, University of Michigan, Ann Arbor, Michigan.

Larry King is Senior Advocate, Advocacy Department, Western Carolina Center, Morganton, North Carolina.

G. Ronald Neufeld is Co-Director of Developmental Disabilities Technical Assistance System, University of North Carolina, Chapel Hill, North Carolina.

A. J. Pappanikou is Professor of Education, Department of Educational Psychology, School of Education, University of Connecticut, Storrs, Connecticut, and Evaluator for Title I Project FOCUS, New Haven, Connecticut.

James L. Paul is Associate Professor and Director of Graduate Studies, Division of Special Education, School of Education, and Director of Training, Developmental Disabilities Technical Assistance System, University of North Carolina, Chapel Hill, North Carolina.

John W. Pelosi is Assistant Professor of Education, Division of Special Education, School of Education, and Associate Director of Planning and Evaluation, Developmental Disabilities Technical Assistance System, University of North Carolina, Chapel Hill, North Carolina.

J. Iverson Riddle is Director of the Western Carolina Center, Morganton, North Carolina, and President of the National Association of Public Residential Facilities for the Mentally Retarded.

Donald E. Taylor is Assistant Secretary, Department of Human Resources, and Executive Director of the North Carolina Office for Children, Raleigh, North Carolina.

Preface

THIS BOOK IS WRITTEN for all who wish to improve the circumstances for our children in public institutions. The writers accept the view that our institutions are failing our children. Therefore considerable attention is devoted to understanding the nature of the problems faced in providing public institutionalized services for all children.

Plenty of literature exists on psychological and educational morbidity in children. There is ample literature depicting the starkness of psychologically impoverished settings and the impact of these settings on youth. More important than familiarity with the literature that "tells it like it is"—where "it" is bad—is personal sensitivity to the problems faced by today's youth in the educational system or other systems providing services. Parents are familiar with the problem—when their child has been labeled "emotionally disturbed" and placed in a special class without explanation of what *disturbance* means or what the problems and prospects for their youngster are; when they have spent the evening helping with homework their youngster could not understand even after exhaustive efforts to explain it "one more time"; when their child is waking them again with a nightmare filled with monsters and themes of despair and helplessness. Parents know the problem when they have taken their child to another clinic, which may even involve a family move, and have yet another "expert" opinion on the cause of problems but no help in changing them. In fact, all parents listening to their children's daily engagement with the world are sensitive to the problems. For parents of handicapped children for whom the daily engagement is a losing battle the needs are usually more acute and sharply focused.

Parents are not the only ones listening and aware of the problems faced by children and institutions in the educational and habilitation systems. Another assumption sets the tone and perspective of this writing: teachers, principals, counselors, cottage parents, and others who work in "the system" care about what is happening to youth they are frequently failing to serve adequately. This is an unpopular theme in the emerging radical literature of the seventies. It is not set forth here as a naive proposition claiming that all those working with youth in schools and in institutions are competent or even well meaning. Institutions are corrupting, and, as Hobbs notes in the *Future of Children,* big institutions are bad. Within those institutions, however, are vast human resources that are as oppressed as the youth they are failing to serve. Teachers want to be successful, to be good teachers. One aspect of being a good teacher is caring about the educational success of learners.

Teachers come to know the problems of youth and schools when confronted with difficult situations: when the teacher has worked hard on a lesson and been discouraged by a child who fails to learn the concept; when the teacher has a battle of wills with a vulnerable child and has felt at a loss for a mutually satisfying, face-saving solution; when a child falls behind the class because the necessary individual instructional time is unavailable; when the teacher feels she has to keep a child from acquiring special educational services because to request these services might result in the child's being labelled and placed outside the regular classroom; when a regular-class teacher fails to support the placement in her classroom of a handicapped child prepared for and in need of normalizing social experiences; when instructional materials cannot be obtained because of central office bureaucratic "red tape."

There are many villains in large institutions. The public school system houses and nurtures many monsters. Mediocrity bred by ineffective and inefficient bureaucracy is among the most damaging problem. The contributors to this book have considerable experience, both with the educational system that perpetrates mass social and psychological injustices on children and youth in the name of education and also with institutions for the handicapped that assault the integrity and compromise the liberty of residents in the name of habilitative services. Out of this experience the human potential within the system has been found as impressive as the forces against it. There are many who staff the classes and the cottage who care and are sensitive to the very deep social institutional problems that exist for youth and for adults who populate these institutions. As a matter of strategy, the orientation of this book is to improve what we have, not to burn it. Philosophically this book presents advocacy as one attempt to redeem the human potential within our institutions.

On an elemental level, advocacy is representing or speaking for another person. That, we believe, involves caring about the interests of another person. Many care and are effective advocates. Many also care who have not found an effective means for advocating. Many others care, but the weight of institutional apathy and chronic frustration in their previous efforts as advocates have led them to set aside their caring and become pessimistic about what can be done.

This book is not a how-to-do-it manual for advocates. This book, rather, presents a basis for defining and understanding principles of advocacy and describes some basic advocacy systems.

The first chapter briefly describes the need for advocacy from the point of view of institutional inadequacies and develops the perspective on advocacy that guides subsequent chapters.

The second chapter presents a more specific theoretical framework for advocacy. Advocacy as a way of thinking about problems and interventions is not totally separate from the existing literature on human development and deviance. In order to more completely understand advocacy and to exploit the potential of developing effective advocacy systems, it is helpful to understand children and the complex system of deviance. Advocates are concerned about a "good fit" between children and their environments. In addition to an ecological and developmental perspective on advocacy and its implications for deviance in children, the chapter contains a central issue in advocacy, that of class versus individual advocacy.

In Chapter 3 the focus of the book shifts from defining advocacy and understanding it in a way that leads to activity, to describing an advocacy system. Pelosi discusses four generic components to an advocacy system—monitoring and assessing, advocacy action, management, and community involvement.

Chapters 4, 5, 6, and 7 describe child advocacy system designs. These are not hypothetical advocacy systems but, rather, advocacy systems that have been developed and implemented in part or in total. Pelosi and Paul, in Chapter 4, describe advocacy in a project that focused on school, home, and community. This chapter presents the results of an advocacy study funded to develop basic knowledge in advocacy. Pappanikou's description of "dual advocacy" in Chapter 5 is based on advocacy activities and studies in two large urban school systems. In Chapter 6, Riddle and King describe advocacy in a state institution for the mentally retarded, one of the first institution-based advocacy programs developed in the country. Pelosi, Taylor, and Paul, in Chapter 7, describe advocacy in state government, based on experience in developing and implementing an advocacy system in state government.

These four chapters on advocacy system designs emphasize what is possible in advocacy working with the existing system, rather than presenting an adversarial perspective. All are based on direct experiences with the systems described.

Chapter 8 addresses the question of training for advocates. Neufeld and Paul describe approaches to training advocates who do the kind of work outlined in the advocacy designs.

Chapter 9 addresses the issues involved in developing advocacy systems, including crucial decisions with regard to development.

The final chapter, "Advocacy and the Advocates," describes the advocate and the personal consequences of advocacy work. Advocacy takes its toll. The impact of advocacy is considered along with some implications for characteristics of advocates and advocacy activity.

The book is written for people who work in neighborhoods, schools, and other institutional settings in hopes that the concepts, strategies, and experiences described here will facilitate their individual and collective initiative as advocates within the system. The book is also written for parents with the hope that in understanding advocacy within the system, they may find help in organizing themselves in effective alliances with other caring people in the systems who are sharing responsibility with parents in rearing their children. These alliances are frequently found in school boards, state advisory councils, or human rights committees.

Finally, this book is for those training programs that are preparing professionals to provide services to children in institutional settings. Professional preparation programs have unique opportunities to assist in developing an advocacy orientation to service delivery and to provide assistance in knowledge of ways to approach advocacy. Information contained here has been used in training professional special educators, teachers, and administrators, and in inservice training of regular classroom teachers, special education teachers, and school administrators.

This book will not answer all questions about advocacy for any one of these groups. But the authors hope it will provide information and ways of thinking about advocacy that will promote more effective activities to improve the experiences of our children in public schools and other institutions.

Chapel Hill, North Carolina   James L. Paul
Fall 1976   G. Ronald Neufeld
                                                               John W. Pelosi

Child Advocacy Within the System

The Need for Advocacy

JAMES L. PAUL

INSTITUTIONAL INADEQUACIES
AND THE NEED FOR ADVOCACY

IT IS A TROUBLING PARADOX of our time that the accumulation of knowledge and skills for the alleviation of human suffering has not had a corresponding impact in reducing that suffering. Our increasing knowledge about people and their institutions has not resulted in an increase in our ability to participate meaningfully in the constructive life of the community. Some of our most basic institutions, including family and school, are threatened by divorce, delinquency, dropouts, runaways, and violence at a time when there is increased "participation" in those institutions whose social functions are to contain, repress, and remedy.

The way we rear our children and provide for their general welfare has become a major crisis in American life. While our understanding of the psychobiological needs of children increases, so does the awareness of childhood disabilities despite the fact that we have more community, school mental health, and special education services than ever before. While we have the best-trained teacher corps in schools in the history of public education, a constant exodus of children from the regular classroom continues because of our inability to provide adequate instructional programs for them. Some of these children drop out early; others tolerate the boredom of a non-engaging curriculum until they are old enough to leave school legally. Some fight the educational system and are expelled for not complying with school rules. Many others are halfway out in special classes and other special services which keep them

1

from disrupting the normal school programs but keep them in school buildings. School drop-out rates, populations of juvenile correctional facilities, numbers of children seen in mental health clinics, increased requests for special services in schools, rising admissions of children to psychiatric hospitals—all are strong indicators that all is not well.

Teacher unions are being formed and, in some instances, supporting the teachers' prerogative of refusing to teach a child. Teacher associations are active in advocating the rights and interests of teachers. Cases of the handicapped and extruded children are being taken to court. The right to education and the right to treatment are being established in the courts.

Holt, Cole, Coleman, and others have examined the school and found it wanting for educational integrity. Cruickshank, Paul, and Junkala (1969) examined the school as an educational setting for handicapped children and found the misfits to be the administrators and, in many instances, the teachers rather than the child, who is frequently extruded for not fitting the student role model. Silbermann, in a study supported by the Ford Foundation, describes the school as a joyless place. These continue even though billions of dollars are spent to improve educational programs.

The mental health system has not found an effective public health strategy for entering troubled homes, communities, and school environments for children who are hurting. Albee (1959) has pointed out the economic futility of traditional mental health strategies and the lack of demonstrable positive effect of its procedures. While major attempts have been made to provide community-based services, such as provided by the Community Mental Health Centers Act, we have not been successful in launching an effective preventive mental health program for children, and the incidence of childhood mental disorder continues to rise. While significant attempts have been made to provide services to families in crisis, family disorganization, as indicated by increasing divorce rates, continues to be a major concern of those looking at basic child environments. Child abuse remains a major social problem. Juvenile delinquency continues to increase. Many children are not attending school. Schooling continues to be an insult to many children who do not fit the stereotyped social models (Dexter 1964).

While our knowledge of nutritional and microbial hazards and the prevention and treatment of disease has increased we rank eighth in the world in perinatal mortality, seventh in congenital malformation and ninth in infant mortality. Of thirteen countries listed in the vital statistics report of the World Health Organization (No. 102, 1964), the United

States had the worst record for infant deaths due to brain injury, post-natal asphyxia, and atelectasis. The health picture is even worse for poor children, since the above figures include middle class children who usually have a fair level of services. We do not have an adequate public health program that makes health care effectively available to children, especially the poor. This deficiency in matching our resources to our needs involves, among other things, an inadequate delivery system and an inefficient fragmentation of services. Many children continue to suffer from malnutrition, do not receive food during the day while they are in school, and do not have even minimal medical and dental services.

Part of the problem, then, is our failure as a society to effectively mediate necessary resources to children through our primary institutions (family and school). We have also failed to make adequate provision for the vulnerabilities and special needs of children, including health, mental health, and welfare. It seems reasonable to wonder how much our large and awkward social and physical structures, established to serve children, have become part of the problem for children. The child who is retarded only when in school, the so called six-hour retarded child, prompts this question.

ORIENTING PERSPECTIVE ON ADVOCACY

Child advocacy is a rapidly evolving social movement for children, much as civil rights is for blacks and consumer advocacy is for the American buyer. Child advocacy issues are in many ways much more complex and more difficult to state. Unlike other human rights movements, child advocacy is *for* children rather than *of* or *by* children. Children are in many ways the weakest and most voiceless minority in this nation. Advocacy for children will not bring the advocate political advantage or a banquet to celebrate your victories in their behalf.

Part of the problem in defining child advocacy is in our way of thinking about definitions and particularly our definitions of children. Child advocacy resists the reductionistic thinking of behaviorism. A child is more than the number of times he leaves his seat, the number of times he disturbs the class, or his speed and level of comprehension in reading. He is more than the sum total of behaviors we can specify for him. The child as human, a topic saved for Sunday School and omitted from most professional works on the sciences of child life, is a central concern of advocacy. It is the child's humanness, his rights and value as a person, that are most inalienable, not the frequency of some particular behavior we require. While it is true that who a child is and what he does, that is, who he is as a person and his behavior, are not entirely separable, it is so stated here because the distinction is made in much of the professional literature, if only by the omission of all but the measurable and observable.

Advocacy does not seek an escape from values. Rather it views values as being at the center of the debate about human rights. A society that values health, freedom, education, and decency must find a way to mediate those values to its children.

The child advocacy movement recognizes the increasing difficulty for parents, teachers, and other members of the child's environment to do right by children. Our knowledge of the needs of children and the high standards for child care that are part of our creeds (and are becoming a part of our laws) is not easily put into practice in our transactions with children. The guilt consequences of our failures do not help the children, significant others, or the future success of the transactions. The difficulties and complexities are magnified when the children are particularly vulnerable. The problem is how to (1) make the children less vulnerable by providing an advocacy structure for them, and (2) assist significant others, such as parents and teachers, in having a more mutually satisfying (parent-child, teacher-child) experience with children. There are many different ways to conceptualize the problems involved and hence many ways to formulate some kind of resolution to those problems.

We know that special classes for handicapped children do not generally work in the interest of the child. While we have been successful in satisfying our intellectual curiosity about the efficacy of such special arrangements for children, we have not been successful in significantly altering or modifying those arrangements so that they can be demonstrated to work better for children or so that they can be completely dismantled.

We know that an institution far removed from the home neighborhood of a child is not in his best interest. It frequently provides no more than protective custody for the child, while social workers hopefully work to obtain a better community arrangement for the child. In the meantime, the well-known process of the child's becoming institutionalized is in motion. How do we prevent children from becoming institutionalized once they are in an institution? How do we minimize the need to have children in distant and remote institutions?

Labeling, like institutionalization and special class placement, is another form of scapegoating the child. The label does not tell you what to do for the child, but typically serves only to get the child placed somewhere (Trippe 1966). The label communicates negative or reduced expectancy of the child which then reduces the strength of the educational effort (Rosenthal 1968).

How do we intervene in the primary transactions that produce and maintain incompetency in children? Intervention at this level means that we must get involved in the critical life space of the child, his day to day interactions in the neighborhood, home, and school with his physical environment and with significant others.

How do we effect a better fit between the child and his primary environments of home and school? We must develop multiple strategies to obtain reciprocally satisfying exchange between the child and environment. The burden of proof must be on the professional intervention. The responsibility for change must be shared by the professional and those he or she seeks to modify—teacher, parent, child, and others. What kind of mechanism is required at a local level?

To take seriously the pervasiveness of incompetence is to demand much more of ourselves and of our services. Neither the child, the professional, nor the society can afford the fragmentation of necessary services and program organization that reinforces and maintains the socioeconomic structure and keeps the bottom groups solidly in place ("Cooling Out the Poor," Deutsch 1964). There is no hope for the stars in the subterrain of special education.

The sick, the slow, and the maimed may be with us always, but society cannot long tolerate the mediocrity, careless thinking, and unchecked social dynamics that use human vulnerability to protect the place of the more secure. Complacency in our ignorance of how to help, breastbeating in celebration of small successes, and wailing and gnashing of teeth at our failures offer little constructive promise to improve the quality of the childhood experience.

Child advocacy is a growing social movement that speaks not only to the need to provide more effective integrated services, a message most all acknowledge and support, but it also speaks to the need to defend the child against services, no matter how well intended, that favor the interest of the system at the expense of the child. This is the message we are willing to listen to but find very difficult to hear.

We have lost our heroes in the ranks of the helping profession. The teacher in the one-room school, a respected ally of the parents in imparting certain behavior and ethical codes as well as the 3 Rs, has no contemporary counterpart. The family doctor, as the family's hero in health, who shared responsibility with the parents in the care of the children, has all but disappeared in urban America. The known and respected lawman, who was a part of the community protection system, an extension of, not a replacement for, the family's resources for protecting itself, is now at the center of a major conflict in values. These and other allies to families have faded, along with a decrease in the social structure of community and a loss of the central place and integrity of the family.

The parable of the good Samaritan no longer applies to our contemporary system of human aid (Green 1965). In the first place, the Samaritan today would often not stop to assist the beaten and robbed without being concerned with who was patrolling the road. Second, if the Samaritan stopped, he would take the victim to the hospital to have his *injuries* taken care of (where he might be turned away if he had no money or insurance). Third, if the Samaritan took the person to a place to be cared for beyond his broken bones and bleeding, it would most likely be to an institution that would require at least a partial compromise of integrity to enter (Goffman 1961; Szasz 1964); and, if the victim could enter, it would be difficult for him to escape once he was ready to go.

We may be entering one of the most interesting and complex social dilemmas in the history of human service systems. A major encounter now appears to be between the legal mandate of the system serving the child and the constitutional rights of the child. The case of the vulnerable child has been taken to court, starting largely with the 1967 *Hobson* vs. *Hansen* decision regarding tracking in Washington, D.C. The courts have since been very active with litigation on the rights of children—*Arreola* vs. *State Board of Education* (1970); *Covarrubias* vs. *San Diego Unified School District* (1971). These and similar cases have concerned themselves with protecting the rights of minority children, (see Ross, De-Young, and Cohen 1971 for a review of the law).

According to recent decisions, intelligence tests must be given in the child's primary language; test sections that rely heavily on verbal ability must be deleted; and the norms upon which the tests are standardized must reflect the cultural and socioeconomic influence of those being evaluated. Placement in special education classes must not be done on a long-term basis, and periodic re-evaluation must be provided for. Parents must be given the opportunity to participate in the placement decision with regard to their children, and educational programs must be related to the child's needs. No longer can special education be a dumping ground for minority children; the rights of vulnerable children are going to be protected!

This, of course, does not insure that the educational program provided will be in the best interest of the child. It simply assures that the child will occupy some place there. While we frankly have to admit that we do not always know how to provide a good educational program—for example, for some autistic children—we have an ethical as well as a legal responsibility to (1) understand our services to make certain we are doing more good than harm; (2) develop the knowledge we need so we can provide better services; (3) share responsibility for (1) and (2) with parents; and (4) communicate honestly with parents about the limitations of professional skills when the parents' expectations are more than can be met.

Until we can effectively communicate our human concerns and the level of professional ignorance at which we function, we cannot fully communicate our openness to and regard for our most crucial allies—parents and children. Child advocacy should not become an arrogant banner; it should convey human interest in children and willingness to engage openly in the social mission of doing better by children.

Child advocacy is currently comprised of many notions. It is a developing set of procedures: (1) for removing children from environments which demean or otherwise work against their best interests, such as all black children in a special class for emotionally disturbed in an essentially white school or a Spanish-American child in a class for the retarded because he could not read the test items on the Binet; (2) for involving children in meaningful activities after school; (3) for informing parents of their rights and alternative courses of action when their child is given a special label and placed apart from other children; (4) for informing teachers about an acute crisis in the child's life; (5) for providing special tutorial help to a child who needs it; (6) for arranging alternate living arrangements for children who are locked into abusive environments; (7) for getting existing community services effectively to the child when he needs them rather than referring the child to the waiting list of a "more appropriate agency"; (8) for providing an ombudsman for the child who finds himself in court; (9) for removing children from jails; and (10) for keeping children out of ecological traps, such as institutions.

While the banner of child advocacy is relatively new, most of its intended activities and concern are not new—most of us are engaged in at least some of these activities already. Child advocacy does represent a different way of thinking about what we do with children.

Child advocacy sees the child as an individual with a certain potential which is markedly influenced over time by the quality of the child's interactions with his own environment. The separation of the child as problem from the environment in which the problem is experienced, labeled, and action taken usually only serves to quiet the environment totally at the expense of the child. The child is vulnerable and needs help in growing up. He is not helped by being punished or demeaned for practicing the bad habits he has learned from his environment, for protecting a small vestige of self-esteem, by being stultified by a boring educational curriculum, for coping with an overly stimulating environment in the only way his adaptive central nervous structure will allow, or for failing as a transactor where he has never been taught the rules or art of transaction.

Rather than acting as if the problem is somehow located totally within the child and thereby taking steps to isolate or extrude him from his community, we need to examine the child's environment to identify a means by which he may grow and develop in a positive way.

Child advocacy is an attempt at new alliances of professionals for children, the most notable addition of which is the lawyer. When the child's interest is chronically abused—by executive sessions of professional teams who are long on talk and short on action or by unilateral acts of classroom teachers where the child's differences have no influence in the teacher's behavior—the formal judicial system may be the only recourse to significant action in the child's behalf.

Mediocrity is not against the law, and commitment to children cannot be legislated. However, courts and the legal community in general are finding ways to examine social tactics employed by institutions, such as schools, which result in extruding troubling children. Detroit, Boston, New York City, and other urban areas have examined in the courts the problems of tracking and intelligence testing, wherein these practices do not serve the best interests of the child. In school the child is tried. In court the school is the defendant. One wonders, if there were due process and right to counsel for the child in school, would the problem ever need to come to the civil courts?

In a real sense, child advocacy is a social movement directed to the rights of children. It has social and philosophical roots similar to other human advocacy and rights protection movements, such as consumer advocacy and civil rights. Advocacy shifts the focus from the problem of the child and the professional discipline or agency most likely to succeed in alleviating the problem to the child's rights as a person and the legal assurance of those rights. Child advocacy is a way to negotiate in the interest of the child in those instances where the child becomes the problem fitted to our solutions.

In general, child advocacy is a developing methodology for making our child-rearing and special child-serving institutions and practices at least partially accountable to the child. While it may become necessary to confront our child-serving agencies through legal advocacy, the stance taken here is that such confrontation should occur only as a last resort. Child advocacy is oriented to assisting in negotiations between children, the adults who interact with children, and the system.

Successful advocacy in economic, environmental, and legislative areas should preclude the necessity for adversary proceedings in the judicial system. Our experience at present, however, suggests that advocacy is needed simultaneously in all of these areas. While litigation continues to be the least attractive area to many, there can be no doubt of the power of this option in changing the system. This is both a direct change centered on the issue involved and a change brought about indirectly by the anxiety aroused by the potential of litigation. Here the medium is really the message.

State, regional, and even city child advocacy councils can serve critical functions with the large systems of government and services. At best, however, these councils can provide a support structure for the direct work with children at the local advocacy level. They are too far removed to do more. Nevertheless, it is clear that, to be effective, child advocacy must exist at a number of different levels and, at least in the beginning, point in a number of different directions. There is much yet to be learned about advocacy.

Chapter 2 describes a framework for understanding the ways in which institutions fail to serve the interests of children. An interactional perspective is proposed as a basis for understanding deviance and institutional interventions. This perspective and the operational implications it suggests guide the development of the advocacy philosophy and the program designs described in this volume.

REFERENCES

Adams, P. L., and McDonald, N. R. "Clinical Cooling Out of Poor People." *American Journal of Orthopsychiatry* 38 (1968): 457–63.

Albee, G. W. *Mental Health Manpower Trends.* New York: Basic Books, 1956.

Cruickshank, W.; Paul, J. L.; Junkala, J. *Misfits in the Public Schools.* Syracuse: Syracuse University Press, 1969.

Deutsch, J. P. "The Disadvantaged Child and the Learning Process." In *Mental Health of the Poor,* edited by Frank Riessman, Jerome Cohen, and Arthur Pearl. New York: Free Press, 1964.

Dexter, L. W. *Tyranny of Schooling.* New York: Basic Books, 1964.

Goffman, E. *Asylums.* Garden City, N.Y.: Anchor Books, 1961.

Green, T. Unpublished manuscript, Syracuse University, 1965.

Rosenthal, R., and Jacobson, L. *Pygmalion in the Classroom.* New York: Holt, Rinehart and Winston, 1968.

Ross, S. L., Jr., et al. "Confrontation: Special Education Placement and the Law." *Exceptional Children* 38(1)(1971): 5–12.

Silberman, C. E. *Crisis in the Classroom: The Remaking of American Education.* New York: Random House, 1970.

Szasz, T. S. *The Myth of Mental Illness.* New York: Hoeber-Harper, 1964.

Trippe, M. J. "Educational Therapy." In *Educational Therapy,* edited by J. Hellmuth. Seattle: B. Straub and J. Hellmuth, 1966.

2

A Framework for Understanding Advocacy

JAMES L. PAUL

AN ECOLOGICAL AND DEVELOPMENTAL PERSPECTIVE

E COLOGICAL THEORY is not a theory of man but a theory of interaction. It has no static components such as a unit of human behavior but rather examines the dynamic social exchange of which behavior
is a part. Deviance is not reducible to an individual difference but is
rather a register of discomfort or disorder in a social system.

There is a significant positive correlation between the complex social
and economic patterns that emerge with population growth and the complexity of socializing children for that world. The world of which they are
expected to become a part is complex and dynamic. It is changing along
the dimension of social expectation for satisfactory adjustment, and
changing with reference to the behaviors required for survival. We have
not, as a society, kept pace in social changes concerning the provisions we
make for children to learn about themselves and the world. The roles of
institutions change, including the role of the family in rearing children.
As Bronfrenbrenner (1970) points out, "children used to be brought up
by their parents." The reduction of time parents have with children, the
disappearing extended family, the disengagement of the small town and
neighborhood ecology, the age segregation, and so forth have shifted the
home base for socializing children. The vacuum created by the loss of
family strength in influencing, for example, the character development of
children has not been explicitly filled by another institution.

Social change reflects the developing systemness of the world. Vir-

11

tually all aspects of our lives are affected by it. Dubos (1968) writes that even the nutritional requirements change as the life styles of individuals in the society change. Good diet under one cultural condition may not be good diet under another. The dynamic pattern of physiological adaptation of the organism to society is certainly not more delicate than the psychological vulnerabilities of the organism.

From the moment of birth, the child is learning to cope. He brings to that learning a certain genetic potential and apparently phylogenetic characteristics such as aggression, sexuality, and a need for a territory or place. In addition, certain general psychological principles have been useful in understanding the needs of the child. These include the need to feel good about himself and to experience his environment as well as his body as basically dependable in their functions. When these occur in a sufficiently consistent manner, concepts can be learned and successfully applied. He must learn to trust a world that will provide him with information for the environment. The experience of competence and the feeling of worth are psychologically inseparable.

Both the child and the environment have the common urge to survive. They are on different footing, however, to work out the basis for survival.

The fulfillment of the possibilities which are included in the child's genetic blueprint are minimized or maximized by the environments or human arrangements which engage the child's growth. A "fit" between the requirements of the child's blueprint and his environments provides the child with opportunity for maximum growth. When there is a "misfit" between blueprint and arrangements, there is trouble for both the child and his environment in the agitated exchange which evolves. This trouble is often resolved by the eventual extrusion of the child from the environment to endure a calm in the transactions in that environment. Our failure to design arrangements which maximize the blueprinted potential of children and our extrusion by default of many children from the arrangements (family, school, etc.) on which they are most dependent for their required fits, are the basic problems faced by those responsible for what is happening to children.

The problem which we in mental health fields call "childhood emotional disturbance" can be described as the trouble or agitation which results from misfits between child and arrangements. It has created great suffering and frustration for children, parents, teachers, and other community members. We have struggled with the problem for a long time and have developed many alternative institutions for dealing with it. We have seen it at various times, and even currently, from several different perspectives. A part of it is or has been called delinquency or discordant behavior and is handled within the correctional structures or facilities. Another part may be seen as a learning disability and handled within educational programs. Some view the problem from a moral viewpoint, and efforts are made to bring religious influence to bear. Many see it as sickness similar to physical illness, and treatment methods are designed and carried out.

We have most often acted as if the "trouble" is the exclusive property of the child. Scientists have tried to locate its roots at various times in any one of a combination of substructures of the child. The problem has been reduced to the physiological substructure, the neurological substructure, and even the chemical substructure. Occasionally, we have located the problem exclusively in the child's environment. These philosophical points of view and institutional responses are paralleled by advocacy groups which press for response to needs of particular children or to particular needs of children.

Attention is less frequently given to the social process—what happens between child and environment—which results in trouble and eventually in extrusion. We believe that there is a need for viewpoints, programs, and advocacy concerned with (1) fits between children and arrangements, and (2) the process by which the fit is either arranged or aborted.

The ecological point of view is concerned with man's adapting. It is concerned with the relationships between persons and environments. It is not, therefore, a static model which assumes that by holding constant one set of factors (psychobiological equipment of man, psychodynamic equipment of man, environmental context of man, etc.) and then operating on these isolated factors, we bring about solutions to human problems (Rhodes 1967). Rather, it searches for solutions which are addressed to the constant, ongoing, intricate interplay between people and environments.

The ecological point of view locates human problems in the typical exchanges which occur between the individual and the context of his or her life. It sees the critical "problem" point as existing in particular patterns of interchange between people and the environment. To be more specific, it locates human problems at points of "misfit" in the flow between two separate units (people and the environment) of one single system. It treats the individual and his or her setting or context as a single complex system.

One way of thinking about how the process of extrusion is set in motion by the "misfit" is the notion of a "scanner." An individual or a behavior is "deviant" and thus a candidate for being moved out of "normal" settings only when the individual or the behavior has been observed and so labeled. In this identification process, a scanner looks at behavior and asks first if it is expected and then if it is acceptable. If it is either unexpected, unacceptable, or both, a given behavior is likely to be defined as deviant. In making decisions about expectability and acceptability of behavior and response to it, the scanner uses not only the information gained in direct observation but also data concerning the environment in which the act was performed and the responses of other scanners. Once a behavior has been defined and responded to as deviant, the actor is faced with the decision of repeating or not repeating the act. If the behavior recurs, the actor is most often labeled as "not fitting" and thus moved out of the setting in which the behavior is unexpected, unacceptable, or both. Thus the extrusion which is so often the response to identified deviance can be viewed not as something which exists inside an individual actor but as the result of a process of scanning, identification, and response to behavior which involves both actor and observer.

The position adopted here, therefore, is that it is neither adequate nor accurate to define our task in terms of either problems with or of children, or with or of the environments of children. Instead, our task must be defined in terms of the problems which occur in the exchanges or transactions between children and their environments. Such definition places some strain on our accustomed ways of thinking about and responding to the needs of children. To locate the difficulty in the transactions is to require alternative ways of thinking about and managing child-environment transactions and intervening in those transactions which are faulty or abortive.

ADAPTATION, THE NORMATIVE PROCESS

What is different about one person or a "class" of persons that makes us pay special attention to the difference? What distinguishes between the differences of uniqueness we like and dislike, we accept or reject, we value or condemn? What is it about the difference (from me) of another that relates to me so much that I would get involved in deciding the goodness or badness of that difference?

These questions are beginnings in developing a perspective on deviance. They lead us to another set of questions that must be answered first. These questions involve our lack of differences. What is it that makes us similar to others? What likenesses are so important that we would class ourselves as a group with others? What sameness among people is so significant that we would call it normal?

One area that "links" people together is their common set of needs. A part of that area is the adaptation required of each person in fulfilling those needs. This section describes the areas of human need and adaptation as a normative base from which to discuss deviance.

Life in a particular community is like life in any other community relative to certain fundamental parameters having to do, for the most part, with physical survival. That is, food, water, and air must exist in life-supportable quality and amount. There must be, for example, sufficient protection from natural enemies including extreme temperature and weather, predators, and other hostile forms of life to sustain the evolution of life.

Man has the biological and cognitive ability to adapt to a wide range of environments. His adaptation is an interaction between his genetic potential as a biological organism with physical tolerance thresholds and his ability to make decisions about his welfare in a particular environment. Man can, therefore, survive in a wide range of environments.

This is only part of his adaptation. Another major aspect of adaptation relates to his interaction with a particular environment over time. He becomes acclimatized, for example, to temperature extremes and can live in one more comfortably than a newcomer who has lived in an environment with a different climate. He further adapts to a life style. He learns to make decisions about his food which may be different from foods available in another climate. His body "learns" to accommodate these decisions. He further learns certain rituals, to value certain things, to think in certain ways, and to control his own behavior cognitively in such a way as to survive in culture which has evolved as a collective way of life. The evolution of culture is the history of man's adaptation to others, in a natural environment.

Two needs, then, coexist: the maintenance of physical life and the maintenance of a way of life or the culture.

One of the primary human development concepts is that learning starts at least at birth. The interaction between learning and the genetic endowment of man is essentially after birth. From the point of view of the individual, the development of his body and a way of life that is workable for him and the culture are closely interconnected aspects of his growth into interdependent membership in the culture.

The culture maintains as a more or less dependable context which represents the history of human resolution of individual needs with the human collective and the natural environment. The adoption of a compatible life style is part of a person's survival in the normal life of the culture.

The social scientists have taught us about the nature and evolution of culture and its determinant role in behavior. The behavioral and physical scientists have taught us about the biophysical dimensions of adaptations, including the very complex central nervous system. Now both the social and behavioral scientists are teaching us more about the interaction of physical, cultural, and social phenomena. The ecologists are teaching us more about the essential interconnectedness of all aspects of physical and cultural life. While we continue to think in reductionistic, categorical terms, which is how we have learned to think and talk, we are beginning to learn more about the interactional genesis of behavior and to question certain social and professional processes that have evolved to represent a kind of insular causality.

The point made here, then, is that human beings and their sociocultural context are inseparable, that physical, social, and cultural phenomena are variably correlated, and that the cause of behavior and its effect are both part of the same process.

The following is an attempt to develop a frame of reference for deviance in the individual-culture connection.

THE SYSTEM OF DEVIANCE

Deviance is viewed here as the maladaptation of humans to their culture such that physical life continues while survival in natural settings with familiar activity is publicly jeopardized. It is a recognized discrepancy over time between the expected and accepted behavior of a particular collective and the behavior of a member of that collective. *Collective* here is defined as a human group that has an identifiable boundary. Family, neighborhood, or school would be examples. The expected and accepted behaviors of a human collective are, among other things, related to the collective's perceived purposes or tasks, the relationship between and relative priority assigned to the purposes in terms of the larger culture, the developmental phase characteristics of its members, the publicness or privateness of the collective, its authority or control structure, its relationship to other collectives.

Each collective functions as a type of circuitry involving energy, activity, monitor, feedback, and change relative to its perceived purpose at any point in time. The monitor scans behavior in the setting and informs the collective as to its relative well-being. It is an essential aspect of the collective contract to survive. The monitor is an abstraction of the way the collective understands the range of expected and accepted behaviors. It is as much a part of the phenomenon of deviance as is the behavior it identifies as either unacceptably or unexpectably different.

Part of the behavior maintenance structure of the monitor is its system of response to deviance. One major aspect of that system which will be described here is that of stigma. If an ecologically significant discrepancy occurs, behavior does not proceed as usual. The group or, to use the metaphor, the monitor registers the intolerable difference and searches for an ecologically relevant explanation. That is, the reasons for the occurrence of behavior are more or less limited to the particular concerns or tasks and language of the settings. A child in school is expected to "behave" and to learn. Aberrance in that setting, then, is typically related to the child's behavior and learning incompetence. Furthermore, the focus of explanation is on the source of the "noise." The monitor does not examine its own process of monitoring. Neither does it examine the relationship between what it monitors and itself. The culture violator, not the cultural breach, is the object of explanation.

Once the explanation for the behavior is determined, a label can be assigned to the person whose behavior caused the unrest. For example, the child who is significantly slow in school may be viewed as "dumb" and eventually labeled "mentally retarded." Given a name for the problem the monitor can then run its program of alternatives for, in this instance, the mentally retarded. The label serves to activate available alternatives designed to restore conformity in the collective. This frequently involves extruding the child from the setting.

Stigma is that social means by which groups protect themselves in specific settings. It is a process of cultural quarantine where the rich are protected from the poor, the controlled are protected from the uncontrolled, the sane from the crazy, the normal from the retarded. The particular stigma involved grows out of the history, religion, beliefs, myths, ethics, and morality of the particular individual-culture collective involved.

Four points are made here: (1) the person who has ecologically relevant different behavior is stigmatized for his difference, (2) decisions made about him are primarily based on group maintenance in contrast to child development criteria, (3) the child has no advocate to represent his or her interests and is therefore vulnerable, and (4) stigmatizing involves moral and ethical issues.

A further characteristic of stigma needs to be noted. The process is arranged such that recovery is minimized. Once the person is stigmatized, it is extremely difficult for the person to recover in that setting.

Another aspect of the problem involves our intellectual orientation to the concept of problems. It is difficult to resist the reductionist tradition, which is so much a part of our training as researchers and social scientists. The problem orientation backs professionals into categorical corners in their views of children. The problem, for example, becomes the psychobiological equipment of the child, the child's social history, or bad habits. We build psychometric systems around the "child's problem" orientation. One of the byproducts of this cognitive process is a taxonomy of problems which provides us with labels or special names for the child. These include brain injury, learning disability, emotional disturbance, mental retardation, and some forty-five others. Another byproduct is the logically consistent attitude that the problem is located somewhere in the functioning or organic equipment of the child. This registers the locus of responsibility for "the problem" and the focus of intervention in the child. Finally, we develop special services and arrangements for the *child's problem* or the *problem child*. This view of the child is deeply entrenched in theories of behavior, in social attitude, and, as has been suggested, our logical positivistic tradition.

The sociologist and the radical activist, on the other hand, have allied in locating the problem in the "system." The definition of *system as the problem* ranges from child socializing arrangements to organized professional services. Generally it means most every organized influence structure outside the individual. Behavior becomes the byproduct of "the system" so that "the problem" becomes synonymous with "the system."

Each view has a basic cause-effect logic that serves both to assign blame (cause) and remove responsibility (effect). Neither sufficiently indicates the interactional nature of the problem.

The following discussion is an attempt to further describe the problems of deviance and conformity in cultural terms relative to the interaction of the child, home, school, and neighborhood. The reason for a rather elaborate development of this aspect of the problem statement is that one of the major problems or social conditions creating the need for child advocacy is at this fundamental level. It is this area that we must learn more about if we are to develop effective child advocacy mechanisms and procedures.

THE ECOLOGY OF CHILDREN

Cultural Pluralism

One of the consequences of a pluralistic society is the absence of a clearly defined behavioral mainstream of the culture. There is not one, but many behavioral codes, each appropriate relative to a defined spacetime. Each spacetime is a segment of the culture or a microculture which is characterized more by clarity within that particular microculture than by clarity of relationships between that microculture and other microcultures. The resulting configuration is a complex cultural pattern.

Each microculture develops its own elaborate system for survival. The behavioral codes in each setting become defined with specific contingencies established for survival. Modes of behavior, including language behavior and belief systems, become articulated into a configuration which identifies one particular microculture from others. Sociologists have described in great detail over many years such clusters as habit, motivation, and group directionality on several sociological dimensions such as class structure. Understanding this phenomenon has given us some basis for examining the difficulty children have, for example, when they have been socialized in one socioeconomic system and then confront the shock of another, such as the child reared in a lower socioeconomic group who goes to public school.

So great has been this dilemma that rather elaborate registers of such culture shock have been developed. One such register is the intelligence test developed to explain behavioral discrepancies in public schools.

Such registers have been used as gatekeepers for institutions which represent the presumed main culture stream. The public school is such an institution. As a result of its publicness, and therefore its presumed representativeness, the public school acts as a unifier among cultural diversities. While the children who attend this institution are acknowledged to be characterized by their heterogeneity, the public school advocates for homogeneous instruction and grouping. While individualized instruction has been a way of talking about an exception to this general cultural convergence, heterogeneity or individualized instruction as a way to get at differences in children has been conceptualized primarily as a strategy to more efficiently and effectively realize the homogeneous cultural mode for which that institution advocates.

It is conceivable that there is no effective cultural unity that is a basis for unifying the quite disparate microcultures in the American social system.

The human organism may be said to be "at home" in that cultural microcosm where there is an experienced "match" or fit between who the person is and what the person aspires to do on one hand, and how the person is defined by that culture and the behavior reinforced by that culture on the other. Since the principal purpose of each cultural microcosm is survival, there will be a satisfying even flow in the exchange between individuals and the microcosm of which they are a part when the "fit" is experienced as working to reciprocal advantage. That is, the behaver will most frequently be ignored or elicit negative regard from the microcosm. The behaver is acknowledged and reinforced because his behavior is viewed as constructive and in the interest of the survival of the cultural microcosm or, at a minimum, are not destructive to that survival.

It may be postulated that every microcosm, as a function of its specific design and therefore its maintenance and developmental demands on individual organisms, has a tolerance band or threshold for neutral behavior, that is, that which neither contributes to nor takes away from the collective. There is also a tolerance threshold for destructive participation which threatens the integrity of the collective. The neutral behavior would be more characterized by privacy and exclusive self-interest in which neither the purpose nor the activity has any demonstrable relationship to the interest of the collective. Leisure time in popular terms would frequently be an example of such activity.

Home, School, and Neighborhood

It is interesting to examine such a notion in the polycultural arrangement of the public school. Leisure or recess has traditionally been viewed as a time out from the main work of school, which is a preparation for a role in maintaining or developing "the culture." Such preparation is also described in terms of personal development and growth. That the student would "be a better person" and also a "good citizen" would be an admitted aim of the educational system. This is what being a "cultured person" is frequently taken to mean. The educational process, however, is oriented in the same direction as the public school, the presumed architect and gatekeeper of that educational process—that is, to the hypothetical general culture.

School is a social institution directed in the interest of a convergence hypothesis, namely the general social good. This was experienced as entirely appropriate when the school, the home, and the neighborhood were all parts of the same cultural circuitry. The perceived interests of that particular microcosm—behavioral codes, regulators of process and strategy—were parameters for an intact functional ecological unit. The social conventions for rearing children flowed evenly through the collective in the interest of the desired social roles. This was a very convergent-oriented process because preparation for life (Pestalozzi 1951) was preparation for a more or less specific life in a particular microculture. The evolution of character in such a closed system was not in any sense left to chance as all of the contingencies were arranged to insure the intended social-individual product.

Today, the public school may be the most serious cultural anachronism. Green (1965) and others have argued effectively that the sense of community is dead. The intact cultural microcosms in which the idea of neighbor is as critical to the viability of the microcosm as is the institution may no longer exist. The cultural phenomenon of school as the significant community ally in preparing children for life in the microculture now is in serious question. High social mobility which results in a culturally unstable population in any given place and/or time; increased population; increased knowledge about cultural alternatives in terms of belief and behavior as a result of mass media successes in sharing knowledge about the world; and accelerated complexity in the adult role model alternatives, including technical job options and increased time required to prepare (in school) for "adult life," have all contributed to the extraordinary diversity in culture and the ambiguity of rules for successful participation. Behavioral expectations have become more complex as the alternatives in different spacetimes have been revealed across the cultural microcosms. Wheelis (1958) has eloquently described the psychodynamic consequences for the individual organism experiencing the diversity. It is not surprising that the experience of diversity and disunity should result in alienation and that the general experience of alienation should give rise to a revival of attempts to create "community." Communes, which develop their own languages, dress styles, and behavioral codes may be viewed from this perspective.

The diversity and disunity in the culture, including the dismantling of the "neighborhood school" (which followed the dismantling of the neighborhood), has left character development, preparation for a role in the microculture, and the adoption of an ecology-specific "good life" role model to chance. There is no effective alliance among the child-socializing agents either in the strategy and rules of child-rearing or a shared commitment to the desired outcome of such a process. The diversity may be so exaggerated that no cultural grid either conceptually or in the form of a social mechanism can bring about unity. The school has become the repository of increasing attempts to "patch it into the circuitry of the community." The attempt is to reformulate the mission of the school and from that point to make some sense out of its methods. The recent responses to this particular crisis have been to advocate for heterogeneity in the school, or at a minimum to advocate for the interest of the individual child in the system. Advocacy for the child which draws a line between the child's interests and the self-sustaining interest of the institution has so far been formulated more in terms of constitutional rights than in terms of educational process.

It is not surprising that psychological disturbances formulated in mental health terms have shifted from being predominantly neurotic to being more generally character disordered in nature. It is also not surprising that we are much less successful in coping with character disorder than we were with neurosis. The primary cultural agent outside the home, be it teacher or therapist, is part of the cultural dilemma and diversity described above. The teacher is, by admission, a primary mediator of the culture. In the diversity and ambiguity of the culture's being mediated it is not surprising that the teacher finds him or herself while on one hand the most informed, technically competent, and assisted (by aides, equipment, materials, research, consultation) teacher in the history of the world, the teacher is at the same time the most agitated, uncertain, and anxious teacher in the history of the world. The teacher's stress comes not from the technical issues of education, but rather from the teacher's role as bearer of a culture which the teacher must formulate and articulate among other things through modeling to a culturally diverse classroom with students whose parents known as neither ally nor alien. Trippe has described the dilemma of teachers and their need for a personal support system.

Perhaps the major difficulty comes in the role a culture advocate must play in formulating the case of deviance and an appropriate response to it. Deviance is a well-known, well-formulated, well-documented characteristic of microcultures. Processes for dealing with deviance, such as scapegoating, are also carefully described and have been extensively observed. So predictable and characteristic are such processes that they become part of the thinking of people such as psychotherapists who work with groups of individuals. Differences of opinion, of behavior, or of belief are common in history and have been the basis of major conflicts ranging from wars to neighborhood feuds. When the difference is significant or important enough, conflict arises. The style of conflict depends on the nature of the issue and opposing forces.

The major forces of diversity have engaged in differences that have been important enough to create behaviors and conditions such that it could be observed: "Violence is as American as apple pie." This, however, is a view at a cultural macrocosm level in which the disunity can be observed and the emergent agitation and violence can be described. The case is somewhat different at the microcosm level, such as family, school, and community, where the words are different, but the social phenomena may be quite similar.

By the time the child enters the public schools, he or she has already negotiated certain critical vulnerabilities with the microculture of parents and the physical if not social neighborhood. The child has learned about him or herself as a part of and apart from the world. The child has developed and tested some hypotheses about him or herself and the world. The child has experienced the relative trustability of his or her own body as well as the cultural context in which that body works. Some argue convincingly that the child has already formulated certain characterological patterns which will not be significantly modified by either the experience of school or society. The child's encounter, then, in school is with other children who have had quite different experiences, who may have formulated rather different character structures. Furthermore, the child's encounter is with a teacher who may or may not have some understanding of the progression of biosocial events which have preceded the child's entry into the school, but who certainly does not know the particular variation of those events. The teacher probably knows and may have had some experience with the range of expected behavior of children at that particular age in school. The teacher has the task of accomplishing certain institutional objectives relative to children, usually in a specified age-grade band. If the teacher is well-trained and particularly astute, he or she develops a methodology which connects the individual child's readiness with a realistic level of the institutional objective. The teacher is not just a technician in the classroom, but a participating member of that human ecology or cultural microcosm. The teacher as well as the institution must be satisfied. The teacher can become angry, frustrated, agitated as well as pleased, satisfied and joyous, and can act on the basis of those feelings. The teacher has rules for behavior in the environment he or she controls, namely the classroom, consequences for violations of those rules, and a tolerance threshold for violations, all of which overlap with a set of rules, consequences for violation, and tolerance threshold of the institution. These rules are more or less explicit and more or less consistent from day to day. The typical classroom, then, is a time-limited age-grade specific setting which brings together but does not necessarily unify several cultures and variable experiences within any one culture. There are rites of entry, of place, and of passage. The teacher is a decision-maker who acts as the gatekeeper of those rights—those rights being at any time an interaction of the various sets of rules and experiences and aspirations. The only unity imposed on the structure is that of the institution of the school itself.

The concept of "fit" is a powerful one borrowed from mechanics in examining the classroom as an ecological entity. The environment of the classroom may be said to exist in a state of more or less equilibrium, depending on the "fit" between all aspects of its ecology. Transactions proceed in a way that maintains or develops the setting and satisfies the transactors.

There are several "fits" that could be considered in the classroom. One is the peer fit between the child and other children; another is the child-curriculum fit between the child and the program, content, and methods, and objective for the child; the child-teacher fit; the children-teacher fit; the fit between the child and the physical setting; between the group and the physical setting; between the teacher and the physical setting. The various combinations are indicated by Figure 2.1.

"Fit" here is a concept of positive experience in a spacetime. When a misfit occurs—that is, a negative spacetime experience—it may be ignored, negotiated, or dealt with by a unilateral decision based on the power structure of the arrangement. It should be pointed out that the matrix categories differ significantly in the degree of openness for change and the power invested for significant decisions. For example, in a misfit between the child and the school, change is almost always expected in the child rather than the institution. When a misfit occurs between the child and the teacher, it is the teacher who has the authority to make decisions relative to the misfit. The directionality of the change, then, can be under-

	Child	Children	Teacher	Phys. Set.	School	Curriculum
Child	X					
Children		X				
Teacher			X			
Phys. Set.				X		
School					X	
Curriculum						X

FIGURE 2.1. Classroom fits.

stood in part as a result of this particular arrangement. Institutions remain rather static.

Each microculture may be described not only in terms of the behavioral patterns, interactions, and purposes which characterize the culture, but also by an influence pattern, the predominant strategy for linkage with other microcultures. The linkage network is a message array. In the message array there are signals to counter-cultures or cooperative cultures regarding the rules for affiliatior This includes rites of entry, tolerance thresholds, and consequential recourse to obtrusive difference.

The message array is a significant part of what characterizes the microculture. Such a culture or collective is known principally by its public messages. The legal system is the guarantor of the lowest common denominator of significant arrays in the polyculture. Murder, for example, is in excess of the tolerance threshold of most microcultures. There are conditions, however, under which killing people is acceptable. Defense of person is one of those conditions. Again, this is a value that cross-sects microcultures. There is little stress in the polyculture relative to laws protecting physical persons. On the other hand, there is considerable stress over laws which specify the nature of affiliation of people on a specified land area. Hence, the Supreme Court's civil rights decision of 1955 has not yet been fully implemented. Who attends which school is still a matter of significant social controversy in some settings.

There has been agitation between various microcultures. It is now axiomatic that man's leaving his primary culture does not leave that culture behind. By definition, his transactional style is brought into dissimilar settings. There is, however, ample evidence of a modification of that style as a function of the new space and time in the new setting. The differences between the culture of the setting and the behavior of an individual in that setting and the intensity with which the setting demands conformity are key determinants of change.

The public school is a repository of cultural diversity. The press to reduce that diversity in the public school has been successful primarily because of the ecological management tactics of that institution. That is, the children are kept over time in the school setting physically arranged and scheduled relative to the primary message array of the public school. After a while in a traditional classroom, for example, all thirty children face the front of the room, sit up straight in their seats, listen to the teacher; that is, they look and act and talk like students, the principal role they are expected to play in that situation. When they do not act like students, there are consequences to force them into that role, the only acceptable role for a child to fit that institution.

The problem, then, is to provide the child with some continuity of experience, protection from being scapegoated by cultural wars among the school, home, and neighborhood, support in coping with cultural diversity and developing competencies in tasks for different settings. It is further to provide support for teachers and parents to negotiate their differences and develop more adequate child supportive behaviors.

Community Service Systems

Another major problem involves the relationship of the child serving systems to the community. The sufferings of children have been identified over time. These sufferings have been described and given names and some support generated to do something about the problems. As Rhodes (1967) has so well described in his concept of the community threat-recoil cycle, the resources are turned over to professionals who traditionally have some public vested interest in the problem. Professionals translate the resources into activities of their trade in order to alleviate the *community concern* about the particular suffering involved. This community purchase-of-services arrangement obviously rests on certain assumptions: (1) There is a direct relationship between the services provided and the problem causing concern to the community; (2) the service agency and the system through which the services are delivered are effective in the reduction of the problem; (3) the concerned community requires effective action relative to the problem it has defined.

Strong arguments have been developed which question the validity of any of these assumptions. There is no guarantee of any relationship between the problem that generates public community concern and the professional practices supported to alleviate those concerns. Part of this problem rests in the direction of accountability. Accountability for professionals is usually in the direction of the agency for which they work and the professional organization in which they hold membership. As long as they practice within the policy constraints of the agency or institution and continue those behaviors which either lead to or maintain their membership in their professional body, they may continue to work in good standing.

Another problem that we are beginning to understand better with the development of social systems theory is the momentum in the organizations to become larger and to proliferate their practices. Organizations, like individuals, strive for and move in the direction of optimal states. These states vary between organizations in the form in which they would be expressed. At a minimum, however, survival needs must be satisfied. The primary and, in some senses, primitive drive in organizations is to survive. The survival motivation which is the strongest is naturally attached to the perceived system of accountability.

Neither the typical direction of accountability nor the nature of organizational development provides any assurance that the special needs of individuals will be met.

The second assumption involving an effective delivery system is basically rejected by many if not most professionals working in the systems. Problems such as territoriality, lack of continuity of care, or general lack of access of services to the poor are well described in the literature.

The third assumption regarding the community's demand for effective action has not appeared valid. Major programs continue to be mounted to reduce problems that continue to increase. In part this may be due, as some have suggested, to the possibility that the community's concern (and in some instances perhaps even guilt) is reduced as a function of its having taken some action. It is also related to the lack of mechanism for keeping up with the real payoff of its efforts, which has to do with the general issue of the structure of accountability described above.

ADVOCACY AND THE GROUP: A DILEMMA

Class Advocacy

Class advocacy is the action taken to solve a problem or set of problems for a group of people who have in common, at least, difficulty in this area. Gaining access to educational services is an example of a problem faced by those denied that access. While class advocacy has been effectively used in the courts with class action litigation, the reference here is to a broader context. Class or group advocacy may apply to any and all settings, including the courts.

The myth of class advocacy is the assumption that the individual is represented along with other individuals. The fact is, the individual is represented only in terms of the particular need(s) he or she shares with the class or group. Class advocacy is issue oriented, not individual oriented. It focuses on a problem, not on a person. It has as its goal a common need, not a unique need; what is similar, not what is different. Advocacy covers a wide range of needs but it must keep the common interest and the individual need in proper balance to maintain an advocacy perspective as defined in this writing.

Class action is taken primarily for the purpose of efficiency. It takes too long to do some things one at a time. There are also other purposes such as visibility and the political leverage possible if a large enough class is involved. It is not, however, the central source of purpose for advocacy. Needs are felt one person at a time. Resources can be combined, but not experiences. It is in my experience that I hurt, feel joy, give up, hope. It is in my experience that I must find an understanding of your experience. I know of you what I have experienced.

I have a right to my experience as I have a right to be me, apart, a part, free. My right to have access to the same public resources as others, my right to be treated fairly, my right to live, or my rights as a citizen and my needs as a person—all can be described and, for the most part, institutionally satisfied. They can provide the basis for our being grouped, you and me, together with others. If we have a right that is denied us, we may have a rather specific reason to be together.

Unmet needs are problems. We can be grouped on the basis of certain problems we share. We cannot, however, be put into a class of persons whose identity we share. While our life styles may be similar, our experience is our own, free to change, free from sharing if we wish.

Advocacy for me is support for my freedom to pursue my life, my way, with only those constraints provided either by certain civil boundaries, which keep the exercise of my freedom from reducing your exercise of your freedom, or the genetic limits of my own ability to experience. I experience as a whole person. What I imagine, hope for, or worry about is for all of me. I carry all I am into every dream. What I give up is a cost to my whole self. My integrity does not hurt in a remote corner of my experience when I am demeaned, any more than the hurt I feel when my arm is touched with a hot iron is separate from my body.

My dreams are in my experience. If what I can only dream of is considered a right by all others, my whole experience suffers. All feel their own pain: a child whose handicap keeps him from school, a depressed person whose lack of financial resources keeps him from a "treatment of choice," a boy whose size keeps him always out of the game, a child whose color keeps him out of a friend's home, a person whose inability to see keeps him out of the sight of Jonathan in flight, a person whose inability to hear keeps him out of the conversation, a child whose "no place to go" keeps him out of learning to love. It is absurd to attempt to classify, group, measure, or otherwise objectify and, thus, make community property of the experiences of denial. It is equally absurd to group and place the denied because of what they do not have as given, without option and, in many instances, without recourse.

The point here is simply that advocacy operates on several different levels. The primary level which gives advocacy its mission is the rights of the individual. This is not to criticize other levels of advocacy. It is, rather, to affirm the central importance of individual advocacy and to suggest certain implications of the equation of individual and class advocacy.

Who Speaks for Whom?

One of the most important implications for the distinction between person-oriented and class- or issue-oriented advocacy has to do with politics and bureaucracies. It is commonly held, for example, that categorical representation is necessary on boards and on staffs. This frequently goes far beyond insuring freedom of systems from discrimination. It goes beyond to the point of insuring that a particular form of discrimination, usually political, occurs.

Here is how it works. If we are to organize a board to work on human services for the handicapped, we must have "consumers" or, more frequently, a consumer representative on the board. The opportunities for exploiting the "consumer input" principles are endless. First, what is needed is consumer feedback on how the services are working or not working. "Input" in any generic sense beyond feedback is not necessarily any different for the consumer than for nonconsumers.

Second, consumer representation frequently means one representative. That representative is usually visibly or obviously a consumer. What is obtained is, at best, an individual's views and a report of his own experience. He does not necessarily speak for the class. He certainly does not represent their experiences. He is usually not elected and does not have a relationship with the class that claims representativeness. In fact, he usually has more resources, both personal and financial, and invariably more political support. He represents, if anything, one end of the distribution on certain factors.

He would be the first to know your bigotry when you implied, "when you've seen (or heard) one, you've seen them all." Yet his asking you to accept his views on all topics as representing "our group's" views belies that very presumption.

Even more blatantly deceptive can be the consumer representative, the organizational executive who makes a living representing a class of others. One needs only to look at the records to be thankful that they exist and do the things they do. Class advocacy, even (or especially) when mediated by an organization, has been effective. The point here is that who speaks for the class is a deceptively simple question.

What has been discussed in many quarters is the authority aspect of that question. Who is authorized—legally, professionally, politically— to say the way it is and is going to be? The other major part of the question, however, is: for which class does the duly authorized speak? If individual advocacy affirms that it is the individuality that is most central to the advocacy, it must simultaneously affirm the myth, the hypothetical-ness, and even the misleading assumptions of "them," the group, or the class.

Representation of a class is best kept at an issue level where what is wanted or asked for can be verified by those the advocate says want it. Representatives on boards or committees "speaking for" should be very clear on what, if anything, they presume to represent that is different from others on the board. To claim class representation in all areas does an injustice to the individual personhood of those identified with the class.

As a matter of organizational policy and of advocacy principle, it is preferred that, in all instances possible, a person speaks for himself. Information systems need to be developed with this being, as much as possible, the guiding principle. When that is not possible, the conditions and limitations under which one person speaks for another need to be clearly specified. It is presumptuous to assume otherwise.

REFERENCES

Bronfenbrenner, Urie. *Two Worlds of Childhood, U.S. and U.S.S.R.* New York: Russell Sage Foundation, 1970.

Dubos, René. *So Human An Animal.* New York: Scribners, 1968.

Green, T. Unpublished lecture, Syracuse University, 1965.

Pestalozzi, J. H. *The Education of Man.* New York: Greenwood Press, 1951.

Rhodes, William C. "The Disturbing Child: A Problem of Ecological Management." *Exceptional Children* 33(7) (1967): 449–55.

Trippe, M. J. "Promoting Mental Health in Teachers." Presentation to C.E.C. Convention, April 3, 1974.

Wheelis, Allen. *The Quest for Identity.* New York: Norton, 1958.

3

Advocacy System:
Generic Components

JOHN W. PELOSI

THE DESIGN OF A COMMUNITY-BASED
CHILD ADVOCACY SYSTEM

ONE RESPONSE TO THE PRESENT DILEMMA regarding the delivery of service to children is to design and implement systems of advocacy for children. Any total working system of advocacy should operate at each of the different levels—federal, state, regional, and local—but this chapter is more specifically concerned with an advocacy system operating at the local community-based level where children live and where significant direct action on behalf of children needs to take place.

A system, as viewed here, is a collection of activities and elements arranged together to accomplish a particular goal or mission. The goal of this system is to see that the network of child services is operating effectively to promote the positive growth and development of all children living in that community; to identify advocacy needs of either individual or groups of children; and to engage in action to satisfy identified advocacy needs.

A model of a child advocacy system (CAS) would include the major components needed to reach the goal and the activities comprising them. It would also indicate the relationships between the components as well as the relationship of the system, itself, to the community.

The model could then be put into practice in a variety of ways, depending on the particular characteristics, resources, priorities, and needs of the community or neighborhood in which it was based.

DIFFERENCES BETWEEN ORGANIZATIONS AND SYSTEMS

A *system* as defined here is different from an *organization*. An organization is a formal collection of roles arranged in a hierarchy such that an individual occupies only one role in the organization. Each person performs the tasks assigned that role in relation to other roles higher and lower in the hierarchy.

Here we are not concerned with an organization for at least three reasons: (1) the child advocacy system should be community based and should not be dependent on the resources and professional skills an organization requires; (2) a number of organizations dealing with children already exist but lack the linkages (systemness) to function together for the good of children; and (3) there is a need to identify the activities and functions which should be performed to make up the the CAS (utilizing existing organizations where possible) rather than creating another organization.

As the CAS is not an organization, its design focuses on activities, purposes, and linkages, not roles. In the CAS a person or group may perform more than one activity: a neighborhood group could perform governing and decision-making functions, collect and disseminate child-related data, and act individually as child advocates in local schools. Therefore, system activities described here should not be confused with any single person or group. In one community, certain activities could be performed by a professional, full-time person. In another community, the same activities could be performed by trained volunteers, part time. This illustrates the intention of the CAS master design to give direction and identify activities which *should* be performed. Any neighborhood or community wishing to implement a CAS must assign people to activities in a manner best suiting its current situation. The design identifies necessary activities which must function in concert so that CAS can accomplish its mission.

MISSION OF THE CAS

The mission of a designed system is its long-term direction. The mission of the CAS is to enable and/or facilitate the full physical, emotional, and social development of each child in accordance with his or her potential.

DESIGN REQUIREMENTS

The design requirements for the CAS in conjunction with this mission are listed below:

1. The CAS should be neighborhood based with consumer involvement in policy and maintenance.
2. It should be adaptive to changing needs, priorities and values in the community.
3. It should be capable of being implemented by a neighborhood with few fiscal resources or by one with extensive resources, such that a neighborhood could make best use of available resources.
4. The CAS should be capable of advocating for individual children when particular problems occur and advocating for all children in community organizations and social arrangements.

SYSTEM CAPABILITIES

The CAS should have the following capabilities:

1. It should be able to monitor and assess the interaction between an individual child and his environment to identify advocacy needs and the network of children's services to evaluate the effectiveness of service delivery.
2. It should be able to act on behalf of individual children or groups of children to resolve advocacy need situations.
3. It should be able to involve community and neighborhood consumers, parents, and other concerned citizens in directing, maintaining, and owning the advocacy system.

GENERAL STRUCTURE OF THE CAS

The CAS is composed of four main subsystems or components that work in concert to enable the system to possess required capabilities and to fulfill its mission. This section will include a brief description of each component followed by a description of relationships between components and the community.

Monitoring/Assessing Component

The primary function of this component is to collect, organize, and assess data relevant to system activities. The CAS has need for two basic types of information: (1) child-specific information describing the status of the child and his or her interaction with the immediate environment; and (2) service-delivery information describing the status of the community, its agencies, organizations, and institutions that interact directly with or affect the lives of children.

Both types of information need to be collected on a systematic, continuous basis. It is important to monitor each child as the child interacts with his or her environment to insure that the quality of these interactions is at a growth promoting level for *that child*. It is important to monitor the network of child services to insure that each component (such as agencies or programs) of the service network is operating effectively for children. It is also important to monitor the extent to which the network of services operates as an integrated, comprehensive, efficient system of services.

It is theoretically possible for comprehensive monitoring to be achieved through either individual child monitoring or service network monitoring. Thus, if a CAS has the resource potential to adequately monitor each child, then service network monitoring is achievable. The reverse is also true.

A number of practical constraints usually intervene in actual attempts to use only one approach to the exclusion of the other. For example, if a CAS chooses to monitor individual children rather than the service network, then there must be a sufficient number of people available to monitor each child living in the geographic area in which the CAS is functioning. These people must have both training and time to perform adequate monitoring. The logical candidates for this function are, of course, parents and others close to a child, including friends and teachers. While it is true that much monitoring is already carried out by this group, it is also true that complete, satisfactory monitoring for each child is NOT performed because of insufficient training and time, as well as other even more compelling factors. If individual child monitoring were to be carried out by paid staff, the costs associated with developing the capability to monitor each child would be prohibitive. Even if costs were not prohibitive, the strategy of hiring professional staff to carry out the monitoring function would tend to defeat the development of parent/ consumer involvement. Monitoring of children by parents is the parents' natural right and responsibility. Replacing their function totally by hired staff would subvert the successful operation of an integrated CAS.

Another reason why individual child monitoring should not be the only type of monitoring is that it is frequently more efficient to identify some deficiencies in service delivery by analyzing a service component directly. Monitoring that focuses on the service network instead of on individual children also presents practical contraints. First, many agency personnel feel restricted from providing open access to information about their performance. This is true whether monitoring is performed internally or externally. Second, adequate monitoring must be predicated on the availability of solid indicators of the direct effects of service on children. Such indicators have not been developed in many service areas. Third, the nature of monitoring the service network generally requires that information about the effects of service be summarized. This means that information about particular children may be unavailable, resulting in incomplete monitoring. Fourth, it is very likely that some children who need advocacy will not be identified through monitoring the service network because they never enter it in a way that allows identification.

Even though practical considerations suggest against selecting one type of monitoring and not the other, there are also problems associated with performing both types at a satisfactory degree of completeness. A point to consider is that a certain amount of monitoring of both types is already being performed in every community. The long-range effort is to continue to develop what already exists, extend it by mobilizing additional resources, thereby successively approximating the completeness of the monitoring capability. The principal advantage of mounting both types of monitoring is that analysis of information flowing from each type provides a cross-check on the other. This cross-check provides a measure of accountability within the monitoring component of the CAS.

The monitoring/assessing component also evaluates the outcomes of CAS activities to change situations for individual children or groups of children. All information from this subsystem flows to the management component to provide the basis for need determination, action decisions, alterations in goal and objective statements, and evaluating the results of action.

Handbooks describing these two types of monitoring are available.

To Protect and Respect (Pelosi and Johnson 1974) describes a process of monitoring individual children. *A Matter of Service: How to Monitor Child-Serving Agencies* (Holder et al. 1974) presents a process for deciding how to begin to monitor agencies.

Action Component

The action component is responsible for taking child advocacy action.

The action component plans and implements activities designed to alter individual or community-level environments to enable the CAS to fulfill its mission. This action, as with monitoring/assessing, may be focused on intervention with community agencies or institutions on behalf of either individual children or groups of children.

This subsystem is activated when an advocacy need is detected through monitoring/assessing and when the management component decides that intervention is necessary. The decision to act stimulates the identification and analysis of alternative actions which may be implemented to reduce the advocacy need.

Specific capabilities may include the following.

1. The action component may act as the social, legal, health, emotional, educational, and/or economic advocate for an individual child whose situation presents a unique problem requiring special advocacy.
2. The action component may insure that existing community agencies and institutions fulfill their legally defined responsibilities to the children they serve.
3. The action component may stimulate changes in law, policy, procedures, and fiscal appropriations to improve the services, care, treatment, and opportunity for children.
4. The action component may facilitate the introduction of new arrangements, programs, and activities to improve the life circumstances of children.
5. The action component may assist existing community organizations, agencies, and social arrangements to facilitate the re-entry of children removed from the community to distant treatment institutions, to reduce the inappropriate removal of children to

institutions by improving community resources to serve children, and to reduce the destructive effects of stigma accompanying misuse of categorical labeling of children, such as mental retardation or emotional disturbance.

Community Involving Component

The function of this component is to initiate and develop a CAS in a community and to stimulate interest, ownership, and support from community residents for child advocacy. The long-term responsibilities of the involving subsystem include the following:

1. The involving subsystem may insure sufficient interest and participation of community residents so that the CAS is owned by the overall community.
2. It may provide a vehicle for the input of community values and priorities relating to the community's children and the direction the CAS should take to fulfill its mission.
3. It may provide general information and input from the community regarding needs and the development of programmatic goals, objectives, and actions relating to child advocacy and the functioning of the CAS.
4. It may serve as a vehicle to inform the community about CAS activities.
5. It may serve as an accountability check of CAS activities.
6. It may assist in acquiring resources from local, state, and federal sources for CAS development and maintenance.

Management Subsystem

This subsystem is concerned with keeping the overall system organized and functioning and with handling the monitoring and action capabilities. It is concerned with quality, performance, need assessment, goal-setting, and overall system integrity. It works with the involving subsystem to establish CAS goals and objectives.

As it is the nerve center for the system it both receives and transmits information from and to each of the other components. It determines fiscal needs (budgets) and allocates resources to other subsystems.

The CAS integrated each of these subsystems into a whole as shown in Figure 3.1. The integrating subsystem stimulates initial development,

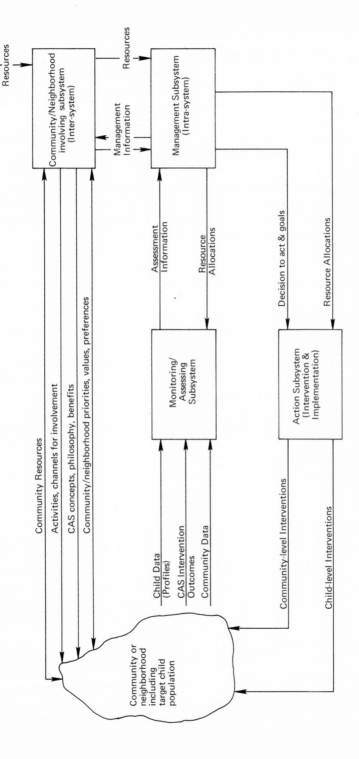

FIGURE 3.1. General Child Advocacy System Design.

provides continuous resources (both fiscal and informational) through community involvement, and provides long-range direction (mission) for the CAS unique to its constituency. Management sets short-term goals in keeping with the long-range mission, allocates resources to itself and other system components, activates system activities, evaluates results in terms of desires, and stimulates changes and modifications. Information about child situations and community situations related to children is provided to management both for need (to act) determination and evaluation of CAS impacts. Management activates intervention when problems (unfulfilled needs) are detected. The action subsystem designs alternative programs, projects, or other interventions, obtains resources from management, and implements selected interventions.

REFERENCES

Holder, H. D.; Pelosi, J. W.; and Dixon, R. T. *A Matter of Service: How to Monitor Agencies that Serve Children.* Durham, N.C.: Learning Institute of North Carolina, 1974.

Pelosi, J. W., and Johnson, S. *To Protect and Respect.* Durham, N.C.: Learning Institute of North Carolina, 1974.

4

Advocacy in Home,
School, and Community:
Child Advocacy System Design

JOHN W. PELOSI
JAMES L. PAUL

PURPOSES AND GOALS OF THE
CHILD ADVOCACY SYSTEM PROJECT

THE CHILD ADVOCACY SYSTEM PROJECT began as a result of concern for children. Concern was based in the recognition that the child service delivery system, including both formal and informal structures, was not effective for large numbers of children.

The following sections describe various aspects of this concern and the preliminary thinking about the relationship of child advocacy to it. The underlying assumptions guiding the development of the project are presented. The purposes and goals and a brief description of the general project design are included, together with a short discussion about selection of a site in which to carry out the project.

Both theoretical and methodological interests stimulated the development of the child advocacy system project. There was the need to consider more useful ways of understanding what is wrong, or what is missing, as well as how to improve circumstances for children. Several major problems provided an orientating perspective in developing the advocacy system. Those problems are outlined below as positive statements of purpose:

41

1. To find more effective means of supporting the positive microculture of the child.
2. To learn more about the primary transactions in the child's ecology where problems in adaptations arise.
3. To formulate a more effective response to the child and his ecology based on that learning.
4. To reduce ecological trappings such as labeling, misuse of special classes, and waiting lists.
5. To re-examine and, where possible, integrate our knowledge and theories of deviance with ecologically specific processes of socialization to the end that we can:
   a. better understand the phenomenon of social deviance, extrusion, and isolation;
   b. develop a more sound research strategy relative to efficient interventions;
   c. develop a more effective and efficient strategy for and content of training;
   d. develop bases for the more precise prediction of difficulties relative to the workings of the child's ecology and thereby the ability to effect preventive procedures.
6. To demythologize concepts of child disorder such as emotional disturbance by better understanding the behavior and ecology of the child so labeled and by parent and teacher education.
7. To develop a means whereby responsibility for interventions, evaluation and resource allocation can be shared with consumers—parents and children.
8. To effectively coordinate and, where possible, integrate professional services for children.

Obviously these kinds of statements could serve only as guidelines. There remained the more specific focus of those guidelines into operational terms. The following section describes nine goals and the rationale for each. The goal statements should help the reader understand the end-states sought by the project. The accompanying rationale should help the reader understand why the end-states were sought.

Monitor Child and Environmental Fits to Maximize Child Potential and Environmental Integrity

There currently exist a limited number of environments for children. Having placed so much responsibility on these environments (school and home primarily) for all children, the need to know the quality of trans-actions within them is great. To leave the development of children to chance by not knowing what occurs and by requiring minimal (in the schools) or no (in the home) competency in child-engaging skills does not make child or cultural sense.

The community has the right and responsibility for knowing the quality of care for its children. It pays for the "normal" care and for its children if it is ignorant of the environments it supports for those children and what is happening to children in them.

Increase Community Awareness of the Need to Create Environmental Alternatives for Children

Given the developmental-transactional needs of very young children and the kinds of environments currently provided for them, it makes sense to reconsider what is happening now to children before they enter school. Rather than "maintaining" these children in a home and in a neighborhood until they enter school, a community might consider creating environments in which the vast amount of child development knowledge we already have could be used to intervene directly in the learning process. Similarly, there may be environments other than public schools as they now exist which offer more opportunity for growth for older children.

Create Alternative Child-Relevant Environments

Community awareness of the need for alternate environments should be followed by attention to design and creation of new maximizing child environments. For example, regular classrooms in the public schools are primarily designed to give attention to cognitive aspects of child development. New environmental arrangements within schools, within individual classrooms, before and after school, or even in transportation arrangements between school and home could give attention to the affective aspects of the child. School curriculum might be designed to better meet the needs of children from different cultural groups who bring with them to school a variety of values, behaviors, and experience with different reward systems. In short, environments might be designed in which learning goals for children are articulated and pursued in life-relevant terms, i.e., preparation for life and tolerance for ambiguity rather than role learning and certification.

Create Alliances among Families, Schools, and Other Community Interests which have a Primary Interest in Maximizing Child Environments and thus Child Potential

Commitment to both immediate intervention in the extrusion of children from important environments and long-term investment in modification and design implies involvement of those interest groups and environments which are now relevant to children. It seems likely that the effectiveness of their individual efforts will be increased if they join together in an alliance designed to serve the needs of children rather than pursuing special interests, special needs, etc., in separate or even competitive arenas.

Catalyze the Existing Programs

Coordination and integration of existing programs is required both for *efficiency* as that relates to duplicating services and delivery and *effectiveness* relative to the continuity of services and avoiding "cracks" in the service system through which children fall.

Increase Sensitivity to the Process of Stigma and Exclusion as It is now Occurring in the Community

Children are currently found in one of three general arrangements: (1) the typical or usual age-specific environments shared by most children in a particular age range (home, school and community); (2) the typical or special "normal" environments (settlement house programs, child development center, foster homes, orphanages); and (3) the "non-normal" categorized environments for categorized children (psychiatric hospitals, centers for the retarded, special classes).

The third arrangement is that most familiar to those professionals assigned responsibility for working with the excluded child. Yet there is little attention given either by the community as a whole or by professionals who work with such children to how the children are moved from one arrangement to another or what the consequences are for either the child or the social arena from which he is moved.

Reduce the Exclusion Rates in Communities

To talk about managing the process of exclusion is not necessarily to talk about ending the movement of children out of what are defined as "normal" settings. It is to indicate the seriousness of making certain that the child is in that environment which works both to his advantage and that of the environment. Our immediate concern with reducing exclusion rates from school, home and community is based on the belief that the "moving out" which occurs now seldom works to the advantage of the child. The decision to move the child out has cultural ethic as well as professional dimensions. The certified inefficiency of the child as the basis for such a decision must be replaced by assurance that gains in the new child-environment are greater than the old and the losses are less.

Develop Re-entry Mechanisms in Order that Children Currently and Futurely Excluded Can be Returned Successfully to Community Living Arrangements

Re-entry arrangements should be developed to include: (1) matching up the children within transactional settings with people who will provide for their protection and development; (2) arrangements for parents and other parties responsible for the extruded children and their transactional needs; and (3) arrangements for other participants in the extrusion process and in the re-entry process.

Existing mechanisms for getting children out are well developed. We have had much less experience with and have given much less attention to getting them back in. This may be due to the fact that removal of the child is most often in the interest of peace in the environment and getting him back in is in the interest of the child's self-actualizing potential. The position taken here is that the price to the environment which provides more access to exit than to entry for children is heavy.

Mobilize Informal Neighborhood and Community Advocacy Resources for Children

There exist many human resources in communities for children that are usually not deployed. These include high school students, older people, married couples with no children and organizations such as churches and youth organizations. These should provide a buffer zone of support between children and specialized professional services. That is, the natural life structure of the community could, if assisted, serve as a primary level support for children in heading off alienation, stigma, extrusion and other ecological traps.

GENERAL PROJECT DESIGN

Activities

At the outset of the present project, it was believed that effective advocacy procedures required activity at the local or neighborhood level. Actions that were viewed as important included: (1) information or data collection concerning the need for direct service to individual clients, the quality and range of existing services, and the need for additional services; (2) making value judgments concerning the need for service at all levels and concerning inadequate or improper service delivered by public agencies or programs; (3) discriminating information concerning inadequate or inappropriate service provision at the local level; (4) discriminating information of, and negotiating with public programs and agencies concerning the need to improve the quality of service provision or create additional services needed by local children; (5) confronting public agencies that are not adequately serving their clients at the local level; (6) learning about alternatives that need to be created in order to serve local clients more effectively; (7) providing necessary support for persons and programs that effectively serve local children; (8) developing effective lobbying procedures and obtaining necessary fiscal and legislative support for needed services; (9) developing personal support structures or mechanisms to provide direct service to children needing help.

Organizational Response to Activities

The foregoing list of activities fall naturally into two categories: implementation, and liaison and communication. It was believed that these mechanisms were needed in order to accomplish the activities. First, a neighborhood child advocacy council; second, a child advocacy team; and third, an advisory body. Two organizations, the child advocacy staff, and an advisory board, were created at the outset of the project. It was believed that the neighborhood council for children would and should evolve naturally out of social problems and client needs that would evolve and become public as the advocacy project was implemented.

Organizational Components and Functions

CHILD ADVOCACY TEAM

The child advocacy team consisted of four persons, a child advocate in the home, a child advocate in the neighborhood, a child advocate in the school, and a child advocate in the community. The major function of the team was to collect information concerning the interactions of the target population of children with the respective environments in which the children lived. This information was to be used to help understand the interactions of children with their total environment in order to understand the need for case and class advocacy. This information would be provided to members of the Neighborhood Council for Children in order that advocacy actions might be set in motion. Data would be derived from advocacy monitoring procedures of family-child, neighborhood-child, school-child and community-child interactions. Members of the team also were to accept responsibility for liaison and communication with families, community agencies and school teachers.

NEIGHBORHOOD COUNCIL FOR CHILDREN

It was believed that as the need for advocacy actions was demonstrated by the child advocacy team, a neighborhood council for children would emerge around specific problems and needs. It was anticipated that fifteen to twenty parents of children served by the project would be active in such a group. Their role would be to listen to and interpret data generated by the advocacy team, adjudicate the need for actions, provide service for individual children as needed, confront local agencies concerning program gaps or weaknesses, establish lobbying procedures for change and assist in the process of finding resources to provide additional services as needed.

ADVISORY BOARD

A four-person advisory board was immediately established. Their major functions were project policy development, consultation for project staff, program evaluation and review, and liaison with a variety of state and federal programs.

SITE SELECTION

A number of communities were examined before the site for the project was selected. Community characteristics that contributed to the selection were: (1) lack of community based services; (2) support of community leaders for advocacy activity; (3) support from the school superintendent and the local school board for advocacy activity in their school system; (4) access to a local school and support from the local principal in launching advocacy in that school; and (5) the site not be so unique that ideas garnered in the setting could not be transported to similar rural communities across the country.

Since the intent of the project was to implement advocacy within the human services network, it was viewed as necessary to have substantial support from a variety of community leaders. Interviews were conducted with key community leaders to determine the degree of support that they would offer and to find out from whether support could be expected from consumers at large.

DEVELOPING THE ADVOCACY PROGRAM

Phase I: Project Initiation and Development—Year One

The first part of phase I of the Child Advocacy System Project (CASP) included a review and extension of initial planning as described in the proposal. Recruitment of staff also occurred during this period. The community in which to conduct the project had already been selected. However, it was necessary to select a neighborhood within the community on which to focus project efforts. Selection of the particular neighborhood was followed by initial entry of staff into the neighborhood. Entry was followed by implementation of general project design. The general project design was reconsidered in light of first year's experiences toward the end of phase I. Each of these aspects of phase I will be discussed in this section.

INITIAL PLANNING

The very broad purpose of CASP was to learn about the concept of child advocacy and its practical relevance for children living in a neighborhood. One premise underlying the project was the belief that for some children a natural advocacy function was operating satisfactorily, and for others it was not.

The intent was to study the individual children comprising the target population as they interacted with the various elements of their environment to learn about the relative presence or absence of advocacy in their lives. An understanding of how the advocacy function worked for some children was to be used to help determine what structures could be revised or added to the community to improve the effectiveness of advocacy for children who needed it.

This is a very different perspective from that of implanting a ready-made new structure called advocacy into the community. This latter approach was rejected because of several reasons. First, it was not clear what the "new structure" really was. Second, the values of project staff in respect to learning about advocacy as it existed prevented them from feeling they had the answers. Third, even though there were some experiences to guide staff in conceptualizing what the advocacy structure might look like, the design was far from complete and needed testing.

The project and its resources was to be used as a way to engage with the community to learn about how preliminary thinking about advocacy fit with advocacy structures already present in the community, and to go beyond existing structures where needed. The project could be viewed as a mini advocacy system in which to test out the different parts of the system, revise them as needed, and make them ready for dissemination to this community, as well as other communities. It was also important to engage with the community in a way that facilitated eventual dissemination.

It was necessary to observe children directly, and to be able to observe the way in which the community's services operated on their behalf. Community child service programs operate on two levels. One level is directly with children, the other is indirect.

A process referred to as "scanning" was developed in order to observe children and how community services operate directly on their behalf. It was assumed that how the community, and its service programs, responded to children could be discovered through observation of the children themselves.

Direct Observation of Children and their
Interactions with Services

Figure 4.1 depicts early thinking about the scanning operation. A method was needed that would provide information about each child in the target population. The method was to begin by observing the child in his environment, whether it was a classroom, a playground, some special service program or his home. The advocate was to collect data about the child, who the child interacted with, and what the interaction was about. A distinction was made between data and information in order to account for differences in values. Once an advocate got to know a particular child

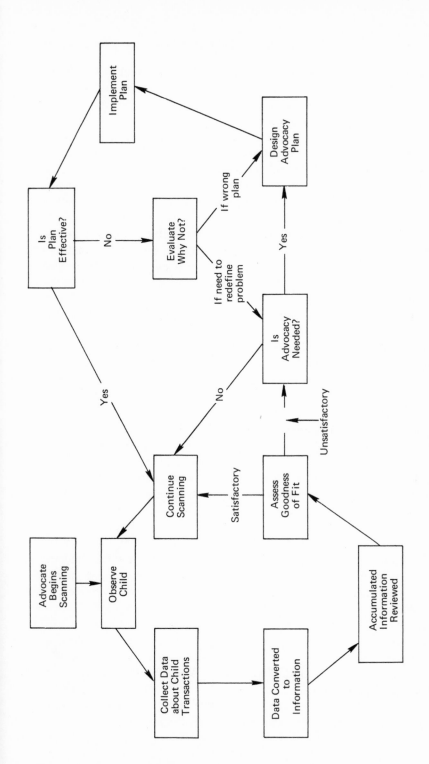

FIGURE 4.1. Scanning Model for advocacy decision flow.

well, and had accumulated sufficient data and information, this information was to be reviewed. The purpose of review was to assess the quality of interaction between the child and the various elements of his environment to determine if change was needed.

If no change was needed, the advocate was to continue scanning. If change was needed, it was necessary to determine if change was going to occur naturally through existing community mechanisms for change. If it was not, then advocacy was considered to be needed, planned for, and acted on until satisfactory change occurred. Once change was effected, scanning operations were to continue.

Scanning was considered to be similar to the observation and assessment operations carried out by parents, teachers, and other significant persons close to children, as a means of determining their level of need satisfaction. It was felt that by using a process similar to one already used by people with respect to children, the task of dissemination would be less difficult than if some highly professionalized procedure was developed.

It was dissimilar from this natural function in that it was to be more systematic, and particularly focused on the child's need for service that was not being satisfied for some reason.

Observation of Child Service Programs at Indirect Level

No specific procedure was developed to systematically observe how services worked at the indirect level. However, one task of each advocate was to assume responsibility for collecting general information about the area to which he was assigned. For example, it was the task of the advocate in school to collect information about the school, its structure, its regulations, its climate, its dynamics as an institution serving children. Other advocates had the same responsibility with respect to his or her area, as described in a previous section on proposed activities of advocates.

NEIGHBORHOOD SITE SELECTION AND INITIAL ENTRY

The superintendent of schools and other people from the community had been involved in development of the project proposal and had expressed a strong interest in locating the project in their county if funding were approved. The project design strongly indicated use of an elementary school as the entry point into a neighborhood for development of a neighborhood-based child advocacy system.

This point of entry was selected for three reasons. First, the school provided a natural contact for entry into the community. Second, the project design emphasized the school as a significant element in the lives of children and thus a vital component of advocacy system. Third, school provided a comparatively efficient means for getting to know children and beginning to learn about their experiences.

The following steps were taken following notification of approval. First, discussion and negotiation with the school superintendent and members of his staff took place during July and August. The elementary school and neighborhood were selected through this joint discussion.

Second, presentation of the project objectives and design to the board of education to solicit their approval of the project took place on September 13, 1972.

Third, discussion and negotiation with the principal of the elementary school took place in August. These discussions involved sharing with the principal, specification of a target population for the first year of the project (all children in the first grade and kindergarten located in the school [N = 70]) and the principal's agreement that the Child Advocacy Team could conduct activities with the school as specified in the project design, pending agreement from teachers of children in the target population took place after school board approval. These discussions included explanation of projected Child Advocacy Team activities within the school in relation to the children in the target population and their teachers. The teachers agreed to allow these activities to occur in their classrooms and to work with members of the Child Advocacy Team.

RECRUITMENT OF STAFF

Staff recruitment began as soon as notification of project approval was received. The following staff positions were filled by October of the first project year.

One of the authors of the project proposal served as project director. The research position was filled by an individual who had had experience and training in special education, evaluation and consultation techniques.

The position of child advocate in school was taken by a person who had worked with elementary schools as a consultant in classroom management, behavioral programming and academic programming. The child advocate in community was a person who had had experience working with a variety of service agencies. She had been involved in developing community-based programs for children and adults. The position of child advocate in neighborhood was filled by an individual with experience in community organization. He had worked with neighborhood residents to mobilize resources to improve community services related to children.

The fourth position on the Child Advocacy Team, that of child advocate in the home, was not filled due to budgetary restraints.

IMPLEMENTATION OF PROJECT DESIGN

During the first months of project implementation, primary emphasis was placed on scanning each individual child included in the target population. The focus of scanning was on the interactions between each child and as many elements of his environment as could be observed by the Child Advocacy Team.

Engaging with the Community

Scanning of the experience of children in the target population enabled entry into each of the four environmental areas specified in the project design. These are discussed in this section.

Initial scanning was focused in the school and resulted in important findings about both the general climate of the school and the need for advocacy within the school. Examples of specific short-run advocacy activity on behalf of children included: (1) suggesting movement of children with poor eyesight from back to front of classroom; (2) bringing a public health nurse together with a teacher to give her information about working with a child with a severe diabetic condition; (3) working closely with regular classroom teachers to develop techniques for helping children in the target population who needed additional support and/or programming tailored to their individual educational needs; and (4) becoming familiar with and calling forth school resources for children, such as reading specialists, guidance counselor, educational testers, and speech and hearing specialists.

In-school scanning of children in the target population also resulted in the identification of several needs and issues for which strategies for working with the school were developed. Among these were: (1) the lack of adequate physical activity for first graders during the school day; (2) a tendency on the part of the regular classroom teachers to apply such labels as hyperactive or retarded to children who were not conforming to the usual classroom standards and expectations; (3) the lack of follow-through on health information which was provided for the school; (4) the kinds of punitive data, "ratings," judgments, etc., which were recorded in a child's permanent school record; (5) the absence of significant parent involvement in school activities, especially among black families.

After a period of approximately two months, project activities were expanded to initiate entry into the home, the neighborhood, and the community.

The process of "getting to know" the children resulted in strong positive relationships between the children and the advocates. Very simply, home entry was made possible because the children invited the advocates to visit them. Advocates found that parents already knew who they were because their children had talked about them. Home visits allowed advocates to: (1) develop good relationships with parents; (2) further describe the design and goals of the child advocacy project; (3) listen carefully to the concerns of parents; (4) set the groundwork for further home visits; (5) begin to explore the possibilities of establishing neighborhood child advocacy councils.

One criticism of this approach to home entry was that it was a slow process. It took about six months to make initial contact with 60 percent of the parents of children in the target population. However, it was believed that slow, careful development at this early stage of the project helped to establish trust bonds important to allowing parent ownership of the concept of child advocacy.

The child advocates, through their association with children at school and in the neighborhood, began to meet and establish working linkages with adults other than children's parents, some of whom shared concern for child advocacy. These adults may be grouped as follows: (1) personnel connected with various projects or programs in the neighborhood (examples: Operation OURS—a program located in the federal housing project designed to provide remedial education for children; home economics training and parent effectiveness training for mothers living in the area; the Blue Ridge Community Action Program, sponsored by OEO, designed to provide a variety of resources and programs to an area encompassing several counties); and (2) "natural child advocates," people not connected to service programs for children through staff positions, but who were known to work on behalf of children in some informal fashion.

The major emphasis, in this phase, was directed toward understanding the neighborhood culture and its effects on children, listening to the issues and concern about children raised by people who live there, identifying potential strategies and resources for development of advocacy activities by the neighborhood, and discussing project objectives and concerns with neighborhood inhabitants.

The primary route of entry to the larger community was through the children in the target population. Thus, if a child was being served by a community agency, a "natural" contact point existed between the Child Advocacy Project and that agency. Agencies were visited by the Child Advocate in Community, using the general project focus of *learning about the nature* of the community service structure for children and how child advocacy might relate to that structure. A partial list of contacts follows: Department of Public Health, Department of Social Services, County (District) Clerk of Court, County (District) Vocational Rehabilitation Office, County (District) Juvenile Court, City Recreation Center Program, City Library Program, a charitable home for children, and a regional school for retarded children.

In addition to official state, regional, county, or city agencies, contacts were made with other groups, such as churches, a group of parents operating a teenage coffee house, a group of parents attempting to establish a "receiving home" for children, a short-term living arrangement for homeless children, and parent teacher associations in the target neighborhood and in the other schools in the county.

These activities led to the identification of several areas of concern and need. Among them were the needs for more foster care situations in the county, especially for black children, for more thorough study and planning in situations of child abuse and neglect, and for short-term alternative living arrangements *in the community* for children who needed them.

Development and Implementation of "Children's Summer Activities Plan"

A major activity of the CASP staff during the spring of the first year related to the plans which were made for target population children in the summer. This activity grew out of several CASP concerns: (1) the identification of needs of children in the target population through scanning, i.e., enrichment experiences, day care, recreation, food, etc.; (2) collection of data concerning activities, programs, and resources available to children in the community; and (3) the need to continue scanning children in the target population during the summer.

During April and early May, members of the Child Advocacy Team contacted the parent(s) of every child in the target population to discuss their plans for their child during the summer and their feelings about the need for other programs, activities, etc. This activity made it possible to gain entry into those homes for which no "natural" entry had been found before. It gave team members a chance to discuss the project to the small number of parents with whom there had been no previous interaction, to let parents know of interest in scanning their children during the summer, and to emphasize CASP's commitment to listening to the concerns of parents and working with them around their concerns. It also allowed staff to identify parent interests in becoming directly involved with children in activities during the summer and the kinds of resources for children represented by the interests and skills of parents.

At the same time that parents were being contacted, members of the Child Advocacy Team contacted those agencies, programs, and groups in the neighborhood and community which were known to be involved with children during the summer or considered potential resources. In addition to providing data about what would (or could) be available for children during the summer, this activity was used to introduce and explain CASP to thirty different community agencies, programs, clubs, churches, and citizen groups.

In addition to yielding information specifically related to summer activities, these contacts also resulted in CASP involvement with several programs and agencies in other areas, e.g., efforts to form a nutrition council.

After these contacts had been made, an analysis was made of needs which had been identified for target population children. Among these needs were day care, enrichment, and recreation. The resources available in the community for meeting them and the concerns, interests, and resources represented among parents of children in the target population were also analyzed by members of the CASP staff.

Based on this analysis, project staff engaged with parents who had expressed concerns about what would be happening to their children and who showed a willingness to work. Effort was directed toward developing more effective activities and mobilizing resources which could be used to meet identified needs. CASP's goals for this activity included development of activities needed by children in the target population, increased communication between parents and the agencies responsible for providing service to their children, increased participation by parents in planning and carrying out activities which were needed by their children, and strengthening of CASP's working relationships with parents and agencies in the neighborhood and community.

A series of meetings was held in the Child Advocacy Team office. CASP's basic role in these meetings was to advocate for attention to the needs of children in the target population and to make available to the group the information collected concerning needs and resources. The group identified additional needs and discussed possible ways of meeting them. Members of the group also shared additional information. As a result of these meetings, parents became involved in several programs on a volunteer basis. Several programs in the neighborhood extended their activities to include younger children. Mechanisms for communicating information to parents about activities available to their children were developed. This activity resulted in increased positive feeling about the advocacy project by parents and other people in the community.

Phase II: Continuation—Year Two

This part includes three sections. The first describes the continuation of field activities. The second describes efforts to design the child advocacy system components. The third section describes decisions made which markedly altered overall project direction. The decisions resulted in rethinking and renegotiating project objectives with the funding group. Instead of continuing on the five-year plan, the project was concluded at the end of three years.

CONTINUED FIELD ACTIVITIES

Changes Affecting Field Operations

The pattern of operation at the project site continued to be relatively similar to that of the first phase except as modified by design work or altered circumstances at the site. One altered circumstance already alluded to was the increase in size of the target population. The original 70 children who had advanced a year in school were included together with the new group of children in kindergarten, making a total of 109 children.

Another change that had occurred was disbanding the self-contained special education class. The eight children formerly in that class were re-integrated into regular classes, providing an opportunity for project staff to observe the dynamics of reintegration.

The increase in size of the target population and the lack of a third member of the team for two months retarded project momentum. Time had to be taken for training once he arrived. It also took time for him to become familiarized with his group of children. Momentum was lost both in keeping in touch with all target population children and with parents and others who had engaged with project staff during the summer.

The size of the team was increased to four advocates in February of this second year. The person hired had been active with the project as a volunteer, and she had good knowledge of the community and target neighborhood. Her skills and experience were helpful to the development of the Neighborhood Council for Children, as well as to advocating for children. These were the notable changes as project efforts continued in phase III.

A number of advocacy issues were identified and dealt with during this phase. Also, other issues, identified in the first phase, continued to be the focus of team effort. Examples of the various kinds of advocacy issues are cited below.

Selected Examples of Identified Advocacy Issues

Four children were identified as involved in bad fit situations in two different classrooms. These were children whose concentration on learning activities in the classroom was minimal compared to the amount of time they spent in activities disruptive to other children and the teacher. They were labeled "troublemakers" by teachers and, because teachers were unsuccessful in controlling their behavior, they had been relegated to a non-student status—teachers were at the point of giving up on them, except to either punish them or exclude them from the classroom.

Team efforts with respect to these children were at two levels. First, the child advocate in school worked with each teacher to shift teacher behavior from punitive to non-punitive actions toward the particular child. He helped teachers increase their skills in managing behavior in the classroom toward productive ends. Second, advocates assigned to the particular children systemically monitored child-teacher interaction to provide feedback to the school advocate and the teachers about the effectiveness of the program. This method of operation was effective in substantially reducing disruptive behavior of each of the four children and redirecting their energies toward learning activities. It also served to increase teacher skills.

Another child was identified as involved in an unsatisfactory fit situation at home. Her divorced mother was under heavy pressure both economically and socially, and was considering giving up her children for adoption. She wanted to give them up because pressures were causing her to act out against the children in abusive ways. The team worked with her to develop and implement a plan providing her with the resources she needed to reduce pressure caused by economic circumstances. Inexpensive day care service for the children was located; she got a better-paying job; and she received assistance in managing her resources through a home economics service. Pressure was reduced and she kept her children.

An unsatisfactory fit situation involving one child led to advocacy action on behalf of children in general at the elementary school. The issue involved the presence of highly negative but irrelevant information in cumulative school records. The school board and administration actually had an excellent policy regarding this issue, together with specific procedures for implementing it, but it was not being carried out. One reason for this was that no internal accountability mechanism had been established. Team effort resulted in getting the school, as well as other schools in the county system, to establish an accountability procedure to systemically implement the school board policy.

The child advocacy team became involved in a traffic control effort when a target-population child was hit by a truck. Basically, the situation involved improving traffic control on a heavily traveled through-street in a neighborhood area with a large population of young children. The team worked with several parents from that neighborhood to effect changes. The parent group and team wanted to reduce the speed limit, discontinue parking, and set up cautionary flashing lights at crosswalks. The outcome of requesting these changes from the City Council was not to reduce, but to strictly enforce, the existing speed limit and to discontinue parking along the street. This issue was not resolved to the complete satisfaction of the parent group and team, but it served to bring positive attention to project efforts, to mobilize parents, and to alert them to the difficulty involved in getting community service deliverers to be responsive to children's needs.

The alertness of the child advocate in school for situations tending to stigmatize school children caused the team to become involved in advocacy action with respect to the school's educational testing program. Initial information indicated that staff in pupil personnel had requested teachers to refer any children who were prospects for special education for testing. Further checking indicated the testing was being done at the request of state education personnel to justify special education teacher allotments to the school system. A check with the State Division of Special Education revealed this was *not* standard practice regarding special education programming. The team coordinated efforts to resolve the issue by arranging conferences and facilitating communication to clear up what turned out to be misinterpretations of procedures at both state and local levels. A situation in which a large number of children would have been inappropriately labeled through testing was averted through these efforts.

At the request of a group of parents of target population children, the child advocacy team became involved in the issue of black identity. Both the elementary school and a day care facility in the neighborhood were involved in this issue. Many black children were served by these facilities, but there was a dearth of programming and materials regarding black awareness. The team worked to bring parents together with personnel from both facilities. The issue was discussed in a series of meetings. Both the school and the day care facility agreed with parent concerns and initiated efforts to purchase materials which would facilitate black awareness programming. Programs involving parents and other black citizens in the community were planned to facilitate the concept of black awareness. Teachers felt a need for in-service training on black history, black identity, and black awareness, and planned to request training from the school administration.

It was noted earlier that children formerly in a self-contained special education classroom were reintegrated into regular classes at the beginning of the school year. CASP staff had an interest in observing the dynamics of reintegration since it seemed clear that there was no careful planning by the school to facilitate this change. The team identified and helped resolve a number of issues relative to reintegration.

The main issue was determining who was actually responsible for the children. The children were dispersed in three different classrooms. It was observed through monitoring that little attention was being paid to needs for special programming. The principal thought the regular classroom teachers were responsible. One regular classroom teacher thought the special education teacher and two other teachers were responsible. The special education teacher did not know. The team worked with the principal, teachers, and special education supervisor to develop a plan of operating procedures for special educational programming for children who needed it. When this was accomplished, a number of other concerns and needs were resolved. Among them were negative teacher attitudes about reintegration, acquisition of special materials, and developing individualized plans for five of the children.

These examples are cited to reflect field operations at the project site. They also reflect the different kinds of advocacy concerns identified by the child advocacy team. Certain examples indicate an advocacy issue unique to a particular child. Others demonstrate how identification of an issue for one child led to changes for larger groups of children. Team responsiveness to issues identified by parents is reflected in another example.

The examples also show different approaches for different concerns. Advocacy action unique to an individual child frequently resolved the difficulty at the specific level where it occurred without the necessity for involving other levels. Other levels were involved if, because of the circumstances, that approach could not work. The team attempted to engage with the system and work within it at the most relevant point where change could occur, whether it was changing teacher behavior through increased skills, helping to develop accountability procedures within the school or within the school system, or effecting communication between classroom teachers, school resource personnel, and state-level personnel.

The preceding material serves as a way to discuss field activities within the context of general project design. The next section discusses project efforts to revise and refine various aspects of design.

Design Efforts

The tasks within the monitoring-assessing component included continuing the design, pilot implementation and evaluation of the scanning process (relabeled monitoring-assessing). Continued effort was to be directed toward design and implementation of intervention methods in the advocacy action component. Work was to continue on the overall child advocacy system design. It was also necessary to design strategies and activities to develop the neighborhood/community-involving component of the system. The following material describes the work completed on each of these tasks.

Continued Design of Monitoring-Assessing Component

The process referred to earlier as "scanning" had proven to be effective in obtaining information about assessing the advocacy needs of

individual children. The early version of the process had undergone a
number of revisions. These revisions needed to be documented.

Figure 4.2 depicts the revised process in flow chart form. Monitoring
of a child began with the advocate observing the child in interaction with

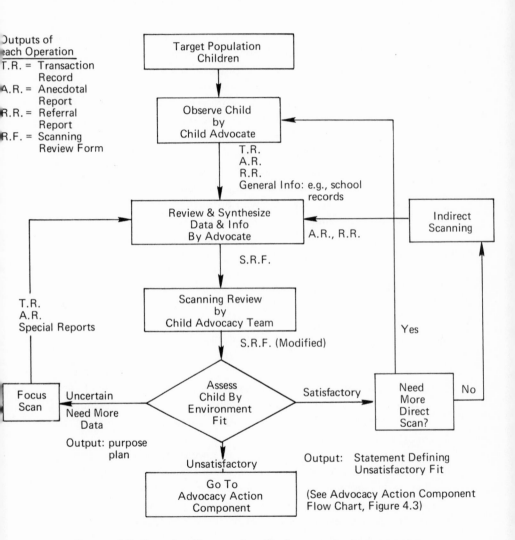

FIGURE 4.2. Scanning Process (monitoring-assessing) component.

the significant aspects of his environment. The advocate also solicited information about the child from sources other than direct observation. For example, information about the child could be obtained from school records, including medical examinations, test data, and other special reports; from verbal reports provided by teachers, parents, neighbors, and others close to the child; and from other members of the child advocacy team.

Monitoring provided a general picture of the quality of interactions between the child and his environment and helped to identify needs for advocacy action. Information was recorded through use of various techniques. Direct observation was recorded on transaction record forms. Verbal reports solicited from others were recorded in anecdotal form. The type of information solicited from others generally had to do with how well the child was performing in school or some other service program in which the child was involved. Advocates also solicited information about the goals and objectives of particular programs for the child where they were not clearly apparent. Occasionally, people close to the child would provide the advocate with unsolicited information about the child. Usually, this kind of information dealt with some aspect of the child's life that was or could become problematic. Unsolicited information of this type was called referral reports and recorded as such.

If an obvious need for advocacy was identified through the information collection phase of monitoring, the advocate set in motion two things: (1) he scheduled a team meeting to consider the situation, and (2) he immediately reviewed and synthesized all information relevant to the situation as preparation for presentation to the team.

Review and synthesis of information was carried out on a scheduled basis for each child. This periodic review and synthesis was performed by the child's advocate. A format was developed to provide a way of structuring this task. Information about the child was categorized as positive, negative, or neutral within each environmental area: home, school, neighborhood, and community.

Review and synthesis served two important functions. First, it helped the advocate to ascertain the extent to which he was keeping track of child interactions in each environmental area. Second, it served as a way of identifying advocacy needs not immediately obvious.

Results of review and synthesis by the advocate were presented to the child advocacy team for consideration. Team review served several functions. It provided an opportunity for other team members to give additional information about the child to the advocate. It provided additional assistance to the advocate in interpreting information that was not immediately clear. It served as an accountability check on the advocate in respect to systematic monitoring and assessing.

The main outcome of team review was the assessment of fit between the child and his environment. Satisfactory fit meant that child interactions were proceeding normally, and were fostering his growth and development.

The team had another decision to make if the outcome of assessment was satisfactory. The decision was related to whether or not direct observation of the child should continue. The decision was based partly on how well the advocate knew the child and his life circumstances. Once the advocate knew the child well, and was certain that life circumstances were supporting his positive growth and development, direct observation of the child was discontinued. Periodic checks were made with people close to the child to assure that life circumstances continued to be satisfactory. Children so designated by project staff were considered to be under indirect scanning. A child was to be returned to direct observation when the periodic check indicated a need to do so because of changed circumstances.

The indirect scanning category was included in the monitoring-assessing process for the following reasons. Direct observation of children was extremely time consuming. The size of the target population had increased from 70 to 110 children. Management of all project activities had become increasingly more difficult. At the same time, the monitoring-assessing process was generating information that was not particularly useful. It had become obvious that children in good life circumstances were supported by the natural advocacy process interacting with the service delivery network. The natural advocacy process was carried out by people close to the child: his parents, teacher, and/or other significant people in his life. There was insufficient need for project staff to maintain close contact with these children relative to the need for work on other project activities.

Unsatisfactory fit meant things were *not* proceeding normally, and that some advocacy need had been identified. In this case, the team was required to formulate a statement defining the unsatisfactory fit situation. This was a step activating team involvement in advocacy action.

It was possible that the outcome of team assessment could be uncertain. Uncertainty about satisfactoriness of fit meant that not enough information was available to make a clear judgment. Lack of certainty could be in respect to simply not knowing the child well enough. If this were true, the advocate had the responsibility to continue monitoring until he did know the child well enough. (This occurred in earlier stages of project operation, or when new children became part of the target population by virtue of moving into the target area.) More frequently, lack of certainty was in respect to specific situations in which the child was involved where the information was confusing, but suggested a possible need for advocacy. Focused scanning was used to try to clear up the uncertainty.

Focused scanning was similar to the regular monitoring process except that it focused on a particular situation with greater intensity. Situations calling for focused scanning required the team to formulate a plan describing the concerns about the situation, and what kind of information would be obtained to clear up the uncertainty, and how it would be obtained.

The advocate assigned to the child was responsible for making certain the plan for focused scanning was carried out. Once the additional information was obtained, he reviewed and synthesized it for presentation to the team and their subsequent assessment of it.

Continued Design of the Advocacy Action Component

Design efforts in respect to the advocacy action process were similar to efforts regarding the monitoring-assessing process. A skeleton process had already been established, partially field tested and had undergone certain revisions. Revisions needed to be documented. This also facilitated efforts to carry out additional design work.

Figure 4.3 represents the configuration of steps in the advocacy action process. The process was activated when the child advocacy team concluded that a child was involved in some type of unsatisfactory fit situation in order to define it in advocacy terms. This usually required identifying the part or parts of the child service network involved in the unsatisfactory situation, and determining whether or not the part(s) were operating effectively. This effort helped to more clearly identify the elements causing the unsatisfactory fit situation, as well as identify elements that might be considered in alleviating the situation.

Once the "problem" was specified in these terms, the process called for generating alternative approaches to problem solution. This step was primarily a "brainstorming" step to think of as many ways to solve the problem as possible.

After a list of alternative approaches was developed, each approach was tested using various criteria. Criteria are reflected in the following kinds of questions: What effect would the approach have on the child? How long would it take? Could all resources needed to implement the

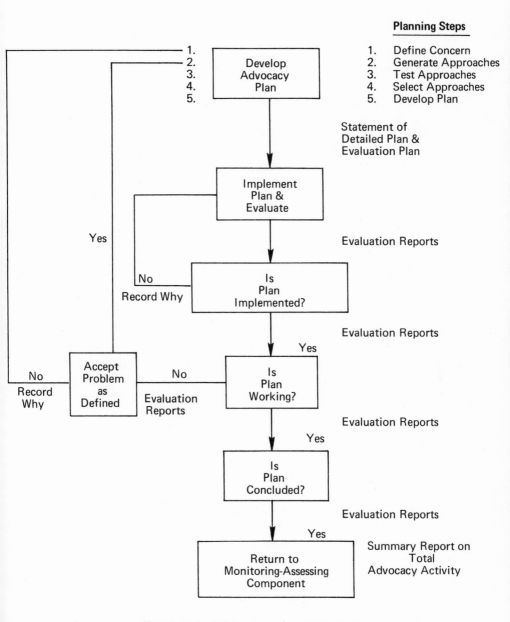

FIGURE 4.3. Advocacy action component.

approach be obtained? What effect would the approach have on project visibility—could it damage community relationships or foster them? Whenever possible, the planning process tried to incorporate involvement of community resources. At the same time, careful attention was paid to selecting approaches that required the least effort to obtain the quickest, most desirable solution. If a problem could be solved by merely calling it to the attention of the person responsible for it, that approach was selected. It was considered more important to solve problems quickly for children than to generate substantial public attention to the problem.

The process of testing alternative approaches usually resulted in narrowing the list to three or four approaches that were considered to be good possibilities. The next step was to select the particular approach.

Once the approach was selected, a detailed plan was formulated to indicate how the approach was to be implemented. An evaluation plan coinciding with the advocacy action plan was also developed. The purpose of the evaluation plan was to make efforts at documentation more systematic, and to keep track of the effectiveness of carrying out the plan.

The output of planning was a written statement of the action plan and the accompanying evaluation plan. Implementation of the plan began at this point.

Various evaluation checks were made during plan implementation. They can be summarized in the three questions found in the flow chart below plan implementation. The first check was to see that the plan was actually being implemented as designed. The second check was to determine if the plan were actually working. If it was not working, efforts were made to determine why. If the problem was in the approach selected, another approach was selected. If the problem was that the advocacy concern had not been defined accurately, further work on definition was carried out, followed by carrying out the steps of planning and implementation.

The final evaluation check was in regard to completion of the advocacy action. Once the operation was successfully completed, a summary report documenting the advocacy action was required.

The advocacy action process delineated in this way provided general guidelines for acting on behalf of children in any situation. The process incorporated accountability checks and the means to maintain adequate records of activities directed toward advocacy.

Continued Work on the Overall Child Advocacy System Design

The purpose of this effort was to continue developing a model of a comprehensive system of advocacy based at the community or neighborhood level. It was felt that by considering the design question, and relating field experiences to it, the major learnings from the project could be distilled into a form that would facilitate dissemination. The intention was not to promote perfect replication, because actual implementation depends on the user and the particular circumstances of the user. It did seem possible to provide general requirements in terms of major objectives, functions, and the interrelatedness of functions within the advocacy system. It also seemed important to show more explicitly how the advocacy system would relate to the child service network.

A document summarizing efforts to develop the design of a general child advocacy system is presented in Chapter 3. It is incomplete, but serves to indicate the direction in which the design efforts were headed.

Continued Efforts Regarding the Design of the Neighborhood/Community Involving Component

Two main tracks were being followed to achieve the goal of designing and implementing this component. The first track was design; the second included various activities of the child advocacy team in the target neighborhood.

There were three main activities under way in the design work phase. The first involved a review of literature concerned with neighborhood organizations, the structure and functions of different types of boards and councils and an attempt to determine the relative success or failure of various approaches. The second involved the analysis of experiences of the child advocacy team in interaction with parents and other neighborhood residents to learn what type of organization made most sense in that community. The third activity involved using information from the first two activities to work out the design of a neighborhood based child advocacy system (CAS).

The function of the community/neighborhood-involving subsystem was to initiate the development of a CAS in a neighborhood or community, stimulate interest, ownership and support from neighborhood residents and general community for child advocacy. The long-term responsibilities of the involving subsystem included acquiring resources from local, state and federal sources for system development and maintenance; insuring satisfactory interest and participation of neighborhood residents such that CAS is owned by the total neighborhood; providing mechanisms for input of community and neighborhood values, priorities and preferences relating to child advocacy and directing CAS to fulfill its mission.

The design problem for the neighborhood involving system was to develop a set of procedures for involving neighborhood/community people in CAS including initial development, continued input and direction, and resource acquisition. Following are general types of activity areas which the involving subsystems should perform, and for which procedures and guidelines should be developed.

1. Initial development of a CAS project. Procedures should be described in a handbook for use by a neighborhood citizens group to initiate and begin development of a child advocacy system in their neighborhood. Included should be background and philosophy of child advocacy, relevant concepts and terms, illustrations (possibly case histories) of child advocacy, and step-by-step procedures for moving from an interested group to an organized and functioning CAS.

2. Neighborhood/community education and information process. Alternative procedures for informing neighborhood residents and the community-at-large about child advocacy and CAS development should be designed. Evaluation techniques for each informational procedure should be included.

3. Regular neighborhood participation. Alternative mechanisms which should be developed to insure neighborhood resident participation in at least two types of CAS activities. The type of activities requiring procedures which must be designed are: (1) Specifying the long-term directions (mission of CAS); and (2) Regular review and evaluation of system performance in terms of CAS mission.

4. Fiscal resource development. Procedures for acquiring fiscal support for CAS should be developed. Techniques for acquiring local, state, and federal government support as well as acquiring contributions should be described. Techniques for grant writing can be included.

The child advocacy team had been involved in activities which provided the idea of shared responsibility for child advocacy since the beginning of the project. Several activities reflecting this were mentioned in the previous description of phase I. The team involved parents in planning for more appropriate recreation programming for a group of target population children. During the program of summer activities toward the end of phase I, a number of parents were organized to meet and work with personnel from different agencies to develop a variety of activities for children during the summer.

Through these activities, as well as others, the child advocacy team gained positive visibility in the neighborhood and made clear their concern for children. They were able to identify parents and other citizens who shared the concerns of child advocacy. They stimulated activities which provided neighborhood residents with experience in planning and acting on behalf of neighborhood children. *These are thought to be critical first stages leading toward the development of a C/NIS.*

A second stage was under way during phase III. It involved the more formal development of a pilot Neighborhood Council for Children. The purposes or functions of this council were stated as follows:

PURPOSES OR FUNCTIONS OF PILOT NCFC

1. Serve as a vehicle for further sharing of project learnings about child advocacy with parents of target population children, and other citizens and groups in the target neighborhood.
2. Serve as a monitor or an accountability check on project activities.
3. Serve as a mechanism for providing the project with additional information about the community and neighborhood.
4. Serve as a means of developing community/neighborhood involvement, representation and ownership of the child advocacy system, its values, processes and activities.
5. Serve as an initial group to consider the means of providing for eventual continuation of viable advocacy activities derived from the project.

It was intended that eventually the NCFC would become the authority which had responsibility for organizing, managing and maintaining the C/NIC. It was to possess decision-making power in its final stages.

It was not felt that the pilot NCFC should possess decision-making power to respect to CASP. The primary reason for this was that the project and its activities were conducted as a function of the contract between the federal funding agency, the agency receiving the project grant, and CASP staff. To involve a third group in this arrangement at pilot stages seemed inconsistent with the existing contract.

It seemed possible that the NCFC could become involved in contract negotiation for the fourth fiscal year of the project. By that time the NCFC would have had a full year's experience. On the other hand, it made sense for this group to focus its efforts on identifying other fiscal resources of a more continuous nature, rather than to rely on demonstration project funds having only two years remaining at best. It was anticipated that the NCFC should become a nonprofit corporation in its final stages.

While the pilot NCFC would not have decision-making power over CASP, it was to provide the critical function of holding the project accountable to the neighborhood. By keeping it fully informed of all project activities, the NCFC would be in a position to serve as a reality check. If certain processes, procedures, and designs developed by CASP did not make practical sense to this group, then the project required modification, or the notion of ownership would have been subverted.

The pilot NCFC was to be comprised of a number of citizens (between eight to fifteen) who were living in or had close contact with the target neighborhood. The following list represented criteria for selecting individuals to participate on the council. Any particular individual did not need to satisfy all criteria, but should satisfy at least half of the characteristics and abilities listed.

CRITERIA FOR PARTICIPATION ON THE NCFC

1. Live in the target neighborhood, or have very close contact with it.
2. Demonstrate a strong concern for children, and have some type of direct contact with children.
3. Demonstrate a positive interest in child advocacy activity either of CASP or in relation to some other program.
4. Possess the capacity for communicating with other neighborhood residents.
5. Serve as a linkage with other people or groups in the neighborhood and community, either as a member of other boards, as an elected official in some groups, e.g., PTA, or be recognized as a significant person to others in the neighborhood.
6. Possess the capacity or potential for working in a group.
7. Possess the capacity for providing constructive critical input to project staff.
8. Be willing to serve on the pilot NCFC and agree to work toward fulfilling its functions.

In January CASP staff finalized plans to initiate the formation of the pilot NCFC. A list of persons thought to meet the criteria for council participation was drawn up. The child advocacy team began contacting these persons to discuss the idea of the NCFC with them. It was anticipated that the pilot NCFC would be formed and begin meeting by mid-February.

Before this effort got fully under way, plans were discussed with the project monitor from the federal funding agency. Discussion resulted in modifying project plans. Rather than formally set up a pilot NCFC as described above, staff would work with neighborhood residents to lay the groundwork for the formation of the NCFC through an election. The election was to be held in September 1973. The purpose of this strategy change was to maximize the possibility of forming a council that was more representative of the neighborhood residents. Another modification in previous plans was what the council would have a policymaking function in respect to the project.

PROJECT REDIRECTION AND OUTCOMES

Modifications in the approach to developing the Neighborhood Council for Children required additional planning. Decisions had to be made regarding whether to hold the election among only those parents of children in the target population, or to expand the focus of the project beyond the target population to all children, and therefore all parents and residents of the target neighborhood. Groundwork activities directed toward holding an election in mid-September had to be planned in order to maximize involvement of neighborhood residents in the selection of the NCFC.

It was expected that preparation for the election would increase time demands on all project staff. Therefore, it was also necessary to reconsider priorities and sequencing of project tasks.

This planning was taking place during the same time period in which proposed project continuation was being considered by the funding agency. It was concluded, at the federal level, that CASP staff needed to reconsider long-range goals and objectives. The outcome of reconsideration and subsequent negotiation between the funding agency and the project staff was to substantially reduce projected objectives.

The project would not continue to work toward the development Neighborhood Council for Children. Two manuals would be produced; the first would describe the process used to monitor and assess the life situations of individual children (Pelosi and Johnson 1974). The second would describe a process for monitoring and assessing the child service-delivery network operating in a community (Holder et al. 1974). Processes developed in the project would then be made ready for dissemination to consumer groups interested in the monitoring phase of child advocacy. Completion of the manuals was to coincide with project termination after one additional year of funding. Skeleton field activities would continue for a brief period in order to facilitate additional testing.

The two manuals were completed during the final year of the project. Additional results are presented and discussed in Chapter 6 on Advocacy Program Development.

REFERENCES

Holder, H. D.; Pelosi, J. W.; and Dixon, R. T. *How To Monitor Agencies That Serve Children*. Durham, N.C: LINC Press, 1974.

Pelosi, J. W., and Johnson, S. L., *Advocacy for Your Child*. Durham, N.C.: LINC Press, 1974.

5

Dual Advocacy Model
for Inner-City Schools

A. J. PAPPANIKOU

THE PROBLEM OF SOCIAL REVOLUTION IN AMERICA cannot, apparently, be resolved by laws alone. This assumption has been supported by the reports of various Presidential Commissions established to look into the problems of American youth and society. These include the report of The National Advisory Commission on Civil Disorders (Kerner Commission Report 1968) and the Report of the U.S. Commission on Civil Rights (Coleman Report 1966) among others.

Attitudes have to change. The National Advisory Commission on Civil Disorders reported that "white racism" and attitudes inherent therein have definitely led to lack of opportunity, hope, and status.

The Coleman Report "Equality of Educational Opportunity," sets forth the various public school and college inequalities of opportunity by reason of race, religion, or national origin.

Elmer Harrison Wilds (1950) states: "Education is the process by which individuals are changed from what they are to what they may become." If the aim of education is to maintain the status quo of inner-city life by not equipping the youth with the relevant tools that are so necessary for social, intellectual, and economic self-sufficiency, then today's educational establishment rates high in the meeting of this aim. However, if the articulated aims are to affect upward social and economic mobility then it is apparent that American educational institutions *must be doing something wrong* if one were to attempt to explain the findings of the above two commission reports in terms of Wilds's definition.

The complexities of the inner city are certainly manifested by the fact that children do not achieve or develop academically on a level consistent with their intellectual potential. Whether or not this is a concern of special education becomes a moot question in that it is exceedingly difficult to distinguish between a non- or underachiever and a youngster who, in time, develops enough negative feelings toward the school to not want to have anything more to do with it. It would appear that special education in the inner city may be equal, generally, to good education and good education may be synonymous with special education. In this context, good education implies that those responsible have to be committed to intervention with the various ecological variables that affect the educational experiences of children.

Before viable approaches to intervention can be formulated, there must be an understanding of the elements that contribute to the "negative learning" of inner-city education. Generally, the inner-city is perceived as a negative entity which has been, and continues to be, separated from the rest of society by social, racial, educational, and economic barriers. While invisible, these negatively perceived barriers are as real as and perhaps more difficult to handle than many physical barriers. While the latter are concrete, the former are both concrete and psychological. Economic deprivation is a physical reality. However, the inner city's educational dilemma is, in many cases, a result of psychological barriers such as low self-esteem, poor identity, low drive, low motivation, and ultimately, low aspiration.

The inner city's invisible walls are easier to permeate from the "outside" (external penetration) than from the "inside" (internal penetration). Internal penetration into the "mega" society, with a hope for some degree of permanent upward social and economic mobility, is very difficult.

While the major variable contributing to this dilemma may still, today, be related to both black and white racism, economic barriers and educational deficits are now also contributing much to this mobility-immobility dilemma in which inner-city residents find themselves. Society respects success and the major measure of success in a capitalistic economy is wealth or economic independence which, in no small measure, is related to educational level. Non-whites earn less than whites and the better educated usually earn more. Thus, for one to be non-white and to be inadequately educated increases the probability that that person will be economically unsuccessful. Such a situation promotes a "Catch 22" cycle for the inner-city individual. This interrelatedness is illustrated in Figure 5.1. It is important to note that the cycle remains intact in either a clockwise or counterclockwise direction.

In the cycle of Figure 5.1 a lack of educational competencies limits earning power which in turn effects many factors which are directly and indirectly related to adequate education. Some direct influences on educational opportunity due to economic deficits are the lack of an enriched home environment, lack of travel, and lack of higher educational opportunity. The indirect influences include a lack of a balanced diet, poor housing, and inadequate role models to emulate. The latter variables serve as an impediment to the acquisition of education being offered in that there is a lack of physical and psychological equilibrium that is essential to enhance attending and motivation and, in turn, learning.

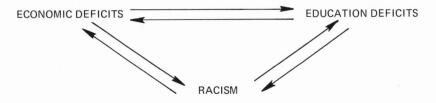

FIGURE 5.1. Self-perpetuating negative cycle.

Economics then affects the number and type of educational opportunities open to youth as well as the efficacy of the education that is offered.

The variable of racism in the cycle acts as a catalyst as well as a rationale for the continuation of the status quo in both economic and educational opportunities. For example, if one perceives inner-city citizens as "uneducated," "lazy," "shiftless," "irresponsible," "unmotivated," or "unintelligent," then to treat these individuals as second class citizens is justified in the minds of the perceivers and the status quo in both education and work opportunity is maintained. Thus, racism serves as a catalyst in motivating some members of society to maintain the status quo and at the same time rationalize and reinforce their actions.

This behavior also tends to engender racism in the inner city inhabitant. The behaviors arising from these emotional aspects of racism are perceived as negative by the non–inner-city society. It therefore serves as added reinforcement to their racist perceptions.

Of the three variables in Figure 5.1, education is the one with the greatest probability for change because it has the potential to equip the youth with the tools that will enhance upward social and economic mobility. These tools not only include academics but also the psychological variables such as self-esteem, net worth, self-image, and, in turn, aspiration. Thus curricular and methodological changes that address themselves to higher achievement and a more positive self-perception should engender the competencies and motivation essential to initiating a break in the cycle. The assumption that this type of cycle exists has led to policies and, in turn, programs calling for supplemental educational funds to Local Educational Agencies (LEAs) by the federal and the state governments for those pupils whose families meet the economic deficit or poverty criteria.

This author believes that the variable which has been most responsible for a continuation of this negative and binding cycle is education. Many have stated that education appears to be committed to the destruction of children and the continuation of the economic dilemma which most inner-city youths face. It is not necessary for the writer to mention any particular city in this presentation but it is sufficient to say that a review of the literature indicates that the conditions prevalent in the metropolitan areas of the Northeast are similar to those in other urban settings of the country.

Tables 5.1–5.4 of reading and arithmetic scores of an urban system support the contention that inner-city education fails in its effort to educationally equip the student. Tables 5.1 through 5.4 present a break-

Table 5.1

Level of Achievement by Sixth Grade Inner-City Youth
on a Standardized Reading Subtest

	Number	Percentage
Four or more grades below	18	1.3%
Three grades below	140	10.3%
Two grades below	349	25.7%
One grade below	245	18.0%
ON GRADE LEVEL	224	16.5%
One grade above	141	10.4%
Two grades above	85	6.3%
Three grades above	40	2.9%
Four or more grades above	116	8.5%
TOTAL	1358	99.9%

Source: Pappanikou (1971)

Table 5.2

Level of Achievement by Eighth Grade Inner-City Youth
on a Standardized Reading Subtest

	Number	Percentage
Six or more grades below	1	.08%
Five grades below	26	2.2%
Four grades below	117	9.8%
Three grades below	191	15.9%
Two grades below	211	17.6%
One grade below	170	14.2%
ON GRADE LEVEL	131	10.0%
One grade above	117	9.8%
Two grades above	100	8.3%
Three grades above	89	7.4%
Four or more grades above	46	3.8%
TOTAL	1199	99.08%

Source: Pappanikou (1971)

Table 5.3

Level of Achievement by Sixth Grade Inner-City Youth
on a Standardized Arithmetic Subtest

	Number	Percentage
Four or more grades below	15	1.1%
Three grades below	30	2.2%
Two grades below	206	15.2%
One grade below	467	34.4%
ON GRADE LEVEL	383	28.2%
One grade above	191	14.1%
Two grades above	51	3.8%
Three grades above	4	.3%
Four or more grades above	11	.8%
TOTAL	1358	100.1%

Source: Pappanikou (1971)

Table 5.4

Level of Achievement by Eighth Grade Inner-City Youth
on a Standardized Arithmetic Subtest

	Number	Percentage
Six or more grades below	2	.1%
Five grades below	5	.4%
Four grades below	70	5.3%
Three grades below	195	16.3%
Two grades below	277	23.1%
One grade below	289	24.1%
ON GRADE LEVEL	166	13.8%
One grade above	95	7.9%
Two grades above	53	4.3%
Three grades above	36	3.0%
Four or more grades above	12	1.0%
TOTAL	1200	99.3%

Source: Pappanikou (1971)

down of scores relative to distance from grade-level achievement for the sixth and eighth grades of an inner-city school system.

The examination of sixth and eighth grade scores does not manifest significant upward educational achievement mobility by inner-city youth. The conclusion drawn from such data is that attempts to reverse the deficit trend and break the cycle are not successful.

It appears that the interrelatedness and interdependence of education with physical and human ecology are as important as any one of these three variables by itself. Thus, most of the federal and state programs relating to increasing the educational proficiency of inner-city youth have included efforts to improve health care, housing, career training and retraining, and economic support. Some ask, "If all this money is being spent, why are the results not more positive?" This writer contends that a formidable, well-planned, and committed advocacy program is essential to orchestrate all of these programs into a successful thrust aimed at a better life for minority inner-city citizens.

The lack of external mobility—the permeation from within to without the inner city discussed earlier—is a fact of life not only for pupils but also for the rest of the inner-city population. It is not specific to any age group. The various formal and informal power structures of the inner city appear to be actively engaged in attempts to effect a continuation of the "worst" of inner-city life if that behavior is self-serving to the power brokers (leaders and politicians of the inner city). This does not only pertain to black inner-city populations, but also to other minority groups, including the large segment of Spanish-speaking Americans. The advocates for these groups may be referred to as "self-serving advocates" of those who advocate for personal gain or physical and/or physical comfort level rather than for the benefit of the student, inhabitant, or consumers. Included are the landlords, merchants, lawyers, architects, educators, physicians, and various local, state, and federal officials. These professionals represent both the private and public sector and attend both to individuals and to the systems to which these individuals belong. Examples of these practices are found in various nationalistic movements. For example, bilingual education has been advocated for Spanish-speaking inner-city youth. However, in many cases such bilingual education becomes unilingual in that Spanish is stressed above English by the community leadership that is nationalistically committed. That youngsters learn the culture and customs of their national origin is very important to the establishment of self-esteem and identity, as well as to the development of ego. But when attempts to attain these goals are carried out at the expense of limiting the child's education via use of Spanish as the primary vehicle for learning, the youth's ability to communicate with the larger society is curtailed. This inadequate command of English and, in turn, unfamiliarity with the customs of the larger environment, results in a greater probability that these youth will fail in future socioeconomic endeavors.

There are politicians who fit the definition of "self-serving advocates," as well as self-proclaimed "experts" within these minority groups; and their actions perpetuate this process. For example, when the politician encourages and supports the "unilingual" and "unicultural" educational program, he does mirror the group's articulated wishes, and thus he is perceived as the group's "advocate." In turn, he can count on the support of this inner-city constituency at the election booth. This process further reinforces his support of unilingual and unicultural educational programs. Another example of the "self-serving advocate" is the "expert" within the inner-city minority group who advocates the "nationalistic" type of educational program, not only for a continuation of the national identity but also to reinforce and strengthen his own position. This is accomplished via the formal and informal power structure of the specific social group and, to a lesser extent, through the larger social set of the larger society. The pressure of the "experts" may be, and in many cases is, perceived by school officials as a mandate to adopt a variety of programs which lack experimental support. Often, neither the self-esteem, self-image, nor the learning style of the youngster is enhanced or improved by such programs. The educator's position appears to be that it is much better to cater to the articulated demands of these groups than to challenge their proposals and engender larger administrative headaches. This lack of educational administrative leadership only reinforces and perpetuates the status quo and precludes any positive advocacy role which might otherwise be assumed by the public school staff.

This is not intended to imply that bilingual programs stressing the culture, language, and customs of inner-city subgroups are not important. However, their emphasis should be consistent with more general education goals. This would imply a reordering of curricular priorities with the major objective of ultimately helping the youth become contributing, self-sufficient, and economically successful members of the larger society. Curricular adjustments that will help inner-city youth to develop into persons who are worthy of dignity and respect and who can achieve financial success and assume social responsibility as well as political power are inferred but are usually not within the realm of reality for culturally exclusive schools. If the aim of "nationalistic" societal groups is to return to the land from which they migrated and establish a power base within that system, then a unicultural curriculum that is often advocated would be in phase with that reality. But within the present reality, where the English language and the American customs and cultures are dominant, this approach can only cause problems for children. The probability is great that they will be less able to adequately function in the environment in which they live. If these children remain in the alien American environment, it is likely that employment opportunities will be fewer and they will have problems coping. In all probability, they will have difficulty benefiting and contributing to the larger society.

Inner-city real estate developers, landlords, and financial institutions can also often be classified as "self-serving advocates" whose aim is to keep inner-city citizens socially and economically immobile. Without the help of lending institutions, apartment owners would not be able to maintain the kind of housing that is so often below the local and state occupancy standards. For example, in the ghetto, rodent infestation is often the rule and not the exception, and there are numerous instances where children have been attacked by rats, occasionally with fatal results. Living in such an environment certainly limits the intellectual and psychological growth of a person. These negative "advocates" continue to exert a major negative influence on the quality of inner-city life even though they face the threat of prosecution. Often they are able to evade prosecution by making only minor repairs. In one specific instance, in a large city of the Northeast, a housing unit was considered by state and local authorities to be unsuited for human habitation. Within a short period of time, following the addition of a coat of paint, these same city and state officials judged the unit to now be livable. Cases like this demonstrate that local and state bureaucracies with the responsibility for assuring that citizens are offered housing which is both comfortable and conducive to intellectual and physical growth are irresponsible, ineffective, and advocates of the status quo. One could say that one of the aims of these governmental bureaucracies is the propagation and continuation of the ghetto. It could also be stated that they reinforce the slogan, "slums are good business." One of the better examples of this lies in urban renewal programs where buildings and land are bought for a small fraction of their actual worth and replaced by edifices catering to the esthetic and economic needs of the larger society. In most cases, this sector does not concern itself with relocation.

The public school sector is equally to blame for its misguided advocacy for inner-city pupils. In many cases, advocacy has been perverted so that the primary concern is the needs of the advocacy group. Busing programs and alternative education programs similar to the bilingual programs previously referred to have frequently failed to meet the educational objectives prompting their creation. Education of youth becomes secondary to initiating the process of the programs. There appears to be a lack of clarity or definition of the educational goals for many inner-city pupils. Statements by seemingly well-meaning supporters fail to take into account the psychological effects upon the youth that they are attempting to help. For example, some "supporters" feel that it may be unfair to place these youngsters with suburban children of commensurate age. They argue that because inner-city children are so far below suburban children in achievement, they would be humiliated and suffer loss of self-esteem and worsening of self-image. This does not have to be, for within normal distribution curves, suburbia has a proportion of youth that are achieving below expected chronological age levels. Most of these youth, however, are not underachieving as would be the case of many of the inner-city youth that are to be bussed. Thus, statements purporting to advocate in fact tend to communicate and reinforce *de facto* segregation.

There is a double standard being applied to inner-city school populations. Pappanikou and Kochanek (1974) found that teacher expectations for inner-city youth are different than expectations for suburban and rural children. The authors concluded that the lower aspiration levels of the inner city are directly related to lower teacher expectations. In an unpublished study, these same authors asked teachers to evaluate specific pieces of work of inner-city youth. Next, these same products were identified as those of suburban youth and were again given to the same teachers to evaluate. The results rendered a higher grade for the work when it was perceived as the product of inner-city youth. This practice leads to false security for inner-city pupils who are led to believe that they are performing well and meeting the school's and society's expectations. Additional data from the same study shows that inner-city youth perceived recitations or the writing of essays as non-problematic. However, the youngsters who composed the norm group in this study felt that these same issues, recitation and essay writing, were significantly more problematic. This study concluded that suburban teachers expected more of their pupils in these two areas than did the inner-city teachers.

Our discussion thus far has centered around an advocacy system which may be self-serving. This is not to say that an advocacy position that enhances the personal and financial status of the individual who is advocating is bad. If that advocacy position is primarily aimed at bettering the lot for the individuals in need of services, then that, in itself, is good and could be described as proper advocacy regardless of the secondary personal gain for the advocate.

ADVOCACY MODELS

Adversary advocacy for inner-city consumers in the 1960s as well as early 1970s has been characterized by confrontations, demands, and boycotts. These approaches have been successful in having demands met quantitatively, but the qualitative aspects of these demands have not been considered. Furthermore, there has been a lack of progressive continuity. In some cases, the meeting of demands was tokenism or a slight modification of the status quo, but it failed to lay the foundation for a lasting major change. Most of these programs were funded with special state and federal project money. School supplies and materials were purchased in great quantity and school systems became oversupplied with equipment. The haste in meeting adversary and, in turn, grant or project demands caused those in authority to overlook the utility and validity of these supplies and equipment and to fail to employ or develop valid programmatic materials and related approaches for the hardware. The educational establishment became defensive and utilized the "shotgun" approach in issues relating to curriculum and methods primarily to "get the wolves off their backs." Universities were not without blame, for they also offered courses that lacked careful research, planning, and validation.

Building an advocacy position solely upon an adversary model failed to produce quality inner-city education. The writer feels that, by itself, the adversary model of advocacy failed to render significant change. At best, the adversary model coerced and forced bureaucracies into some type of action.

The ombudsman advocacy position also failed to render optimum results because there was a lack of clout to initiate, implement, and/or maintain programs that were introduced in response to the demands of the previously discussed community advocacy groups. The major weakness with this model was in the possible intimidation of the advocate who was, in many cases, not the consumer's advocate because he was easily coercible by the school which was paying for his services. Thus, the advocated efforts were neutralized and his role became less than effective.

A combination of adversary and ombudsman models should be utilized so that the above mentioned drawbacks of each may be overcome. It would seem that this dual model would establish and maintain a workable advocacy program for inner-city populations.

Initially, the ombudsman position would force the school and school system to realize that a problem does exist and that the school has to move toward solving it. This function could be performed best by a person within the system. If this effort fails and there is little or no attempt to engender a programmatic resolution to the problem, action based on the adversary model could be undertaken. The participants in this model could be parent organizations, citizens' groups, associations for specific special interests, or any other interested group or groups. This action would systematically render input in an adversary mode and thus more firmly rearticulate the demands initially made by the ombudsman for a specific programmatic effort. These demands might be concerned with school (lunches, curriculum, special classes, athletics), housing (rodent extermination, lead paint removal), or law (equal protection, due process). Once this occurs, the non-adversary agent, the ombudsman, can re-enter the picture to assure that serious planning begins on ways and means by which these demands might be satisfied. The primary responsibility of this "ombudsman advocate" during this phase is to insure planning the proper solution and following it through. The author's experiences, primarily with schools, are that a plethora of programs were and are initiated without careful thought. In these cases, the educator's primary goal is defusing and thus silencing the adversary group. Once this occurs, it ends the advocacy position of the adversaries, for the group's collective ego needs would be met by the apparent success of their actions. These advocates would then move on or be redirected to another problem within the inner city. Many of the programs that were initiated in response to their demands, however, would wither away and die. Thus, there would be a lack of continuity, evaluation, and ultimately accountability, without the ombudsman advocate.

For those programs that were sustained, little thought appeared to be given to evaluation, thus making decisions relative to change or termination nonexistent or at best invalid.

If, as suggested above in the *planned* dual advocacy model, the "ombudsman advocate" entered the picture once the adversaries had forced the bureaucracy into action, then the abovementioned shortcomings of the single advocacy (adversary) model would not have occurred. The ombudsman would follow through on the proposals and make the establishment more accountable due to the clout that would obtain from both his role as ombudsman and his relationship with the other segment of the dual advocate, the adversary group.

DUAL ADVOCACY AND THE SCHOOLS

Initial referral for a dual advocacy program in the schools can be made by anyone—the child, parent, friend, teacher, or any other school personnel. Those individuals external to the school who make the initial referrals are often viewed as adversaries by school authorities. If such initiators of action, whether individual or group, are perceived as adversaries by the administration, then the actions stemming from those transactions are adversary induced and those individuals can be properly called "adversary advocates." If their effort is directed toward the betterment of the education of youth, then they may be properly designated as "adversary child advocates."

Once the initial referral has been made by one of these informal advocates to the school authorities, formal advocacy begins.

The ombudsman advocate has to be a within advocate in that this professional has to be on the staff and his role should be clearly defined as one of advocacy for children and programs affecting children.

There are many who feel that advocates within the school would not necessarily be effective because they would have too much to lose (salary, increments, promotions, and tenure) by questioning the system. Therefore, many feel that they would become passive in sensitive situations. However, if these individuals represent an advocacy movement which is buttressed by the accountability force of the external advocates, they will not be perceived as hostile by the system for they will not be viewed as initiators of demands. Their role would be perceived as facilitative in that he or she will be perceived as an arbitrator who will be child-centered and reality-based as to problem resolution. It is thus assumed that their input would not be perceived as threatening by the school staff.

Referrals that indicate a need for impartiality in problem resolution, due to the following, are referred to the "ombudsman advocate":

1. Unusual needs or demands that appear to be beyond the programming ability of the school.
2. Teacher-child conflict.
3. Parent-teacher-school conflict.
4. Interdisciplinary programming that appears to be beyond the school's responsibility.

Unusual needs and related demands that many school systems feel are beyond their programming ability include most special education related problems for moderately and severely multihandicapped youth. These types of problems require action which may involve facilitating the initiation of in-service training programs for staff, training programs for parents, communication with appropriate parent groups so that budgets may be supplemented, and a search within the system for existing programmatic efforts for the specific type of need.

Teacher-child or child-teacher conflicts may arise when the child perceives the teacher as hostile, dehumanizing, and non-facilitative in learning. The child's behavior in these situations may become disruptive and may be perceived by the teacher as a personal attack. When these perceptions occur, they tend to be reinforcing so that this negative cycle perpetuates itself to the point where the teacher wants the child taken out of the class and the child is overly ready to oblige.

In this type of conflict, the "ombudsman advocate" intervenes initially by talking to the teacher and, in behavioral terms, constructs a rank-ordered inventory of those behaviors which are unacceptable and/or threatening to the teacher's comfort level. The advocate then discusses the situation with the child so that the pupil's perceptions are articulated and known. The child is made aware of the role of the advocate.

The advocate's role is to help the child by resolving these conflicts and getting on with the primary objective of learning. The child is assured that all aspects of the problems will be investigated, and if the evidence supports the child, his position will be supported and programmatic efforts toward resolution of the problem(s) will be initiated. These may include making the teacher aware of the perceptions and/or misperceptions of the child in the teacher-child transactions. The aim of such action is to make the teacher aware that teacher behavior, as perceived by the child, is fueling the negative cycle. Furthermore, it is possible to change the perceptions of the child by a change in teacher behavior and thus to break the cycle. The child is also told that, if the data from the investigation do not support his position, he will be subjected to the programmatic interventions.

There will be times when the formal ombudsman advocate may not be perceived by a specific child as an advocate or person with whom the child can positively interact due to the child's inability to perceive this person as trusting, fair, and one who is deserving of the child's respect. In these cases, the child is asked if there is someone else in that school he would rather have served as an advocate—a person the child perceives as possessing more of the abovementioned advocacy qualities. If the child does select someone else and that person is willing to serve, then he would become an extension of the "ombudsman advocate" and serve as that particular child's advocate, carrying out the advocacy functions.

The parent-teacher-school conflict is also dealt with by correctly identifying the problem areas and the various perceptions and/or misperceptions of the people involved. Most of these conflicts are dealt with in a similar manner to that described above for a teacher-pupil conflict. There will be times, however, when external adversary advocates may also have to be dealt with if the parent has requested their help. In this situation, the ombudsman advocate's greatest tools are objectivity, honesty, and a sense of reality. The author has found in his experiences that such external advocates as parents are, as would be expected, generally more subjective in their view of the conflict. For this reason the attributes of the ombudsman advocate will add trust and credibility and, in turn, render a speedier and more acceptable resolution of the problem.

Two of the most common conflicts in this area arise from special education placement and suspension. Intervention by the internal ombudsman advocate often resolves the issue, circumvents time-consuming hearings, and precludes potential negative perceptions among the participants. A major result from such a successful intervention is a more lasting cooperative endeavor in making the school a more effective place for learning.

One of the better examples of interdisciplinary programming that appears to be beyond the school's responsibility is when parental unemployment leads to parental conflict and ultimately to child neglect. This type of situation is not usually dealt with in terms of the educational effects of these conflicts upon the child but in terms of the general welfare of the family unit. Most of the time treatment of the problems of the principals excludes the education of the child. The ombudsman advocate in such a situation has the responsibility to make sure that the child's right to an education is not abridged by the treatment which is aimed at resolving the primary cause of the problem. Demanding that the child's education is an important agenda item in the prescribed treatment is a major role of the advocate. The lack of advocating for the child's education in these types of situations has, in too many cases, resulted in young children becoming "drop outs."

The adversary advocate enters the picture when, in any of the above kinds of conflicts, there is either a lack or a misdirection of action. As mentioned earlier, the implied possible intervention by the adversary advocate renders clout to the role of the ombudsman advocate as well as providing continuity and accountability for administrative programming.

Figure 5.2 depicts the dual advocacy model, the success of which

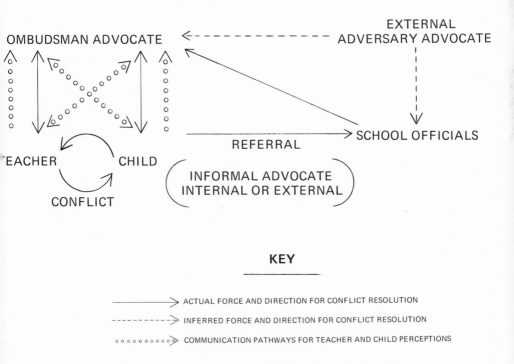

FIGURE 5.2. Dual advocacy model of teacher-child conflict.

can be measured by the degree of interrelatedness between the ombudsman and adversary advocates. This interrelatedness should not be flaunted, but it should be strongly inferred.

If these two advocates are perceived by the establishment as not in concert and/or not mutually supportive, then administrative manipulation may commence. When this occurs in a school setting, the loser is always the child.

REFERENCES

Coleman, J. S., et al. Equality of Educational Opportunity. Washington, D.C.: USGPO, 1966.

Hollingshead, A. B., and Redlich, F. C. Social Class and Mental Illness. New York: Wiley, 1958.

Holt, J. How Children Fail. New York: Dell, 1964.

Kozol, J. Death at an Early Age. Boston: Houghton Mifflin, 1967.

LeShan, E. The Conspiracy Against Childhood. New York: Atheneum, 1968.

Morla, J., and Ramada, R. "The Disadvantaged Child and His Culture." In Teaching the Disadvantaged Child, edited by Sidney Tiedt. New York: Oxford University Press, 1968.

Pappanikou, A. J. "The Importance of Perception in Child Advocacy." Mimeograph. Storrs: University of Connecticut, Box U-64, 1971.

————. "Reading and Arithmetic Performance of Inner City Youth." Unpublished Manuscript, 1971. Storrs: University of Connecticut, Box U-64.

Pappanikou, A. J., and Drake, T. L. "Educating Teachers for the City." Journal of Research and Development in Education, 4 (4) (Summer 1971).

Pappanikou, A. J., and Kochanek, T. T. "Aspiration vs. Achievement: An Analysis of and Subsequent Implications for the Onset of Emotional Disturbance in Urban Areas." In Approaches with Emotionally Disturbed Children, edited by B. Saunders. New York: Exposition Press, 1974.

Report of the National Advisory Commission on Civil Disorders. New York: Dutton, 1968.

Silberman, Charles E. Crisis in the Classroom. New York: Random House, 1970.

Wilds, E. H. The Foundations of Modern Education. New York: Rinehart & Company, Inc. 1950, pg. 3.

6

Advocacy in an Institution

J. IVERSON RIDDLE
LARRY KING

WHAT?

A N ADVOCACY PROGRAM is basically designed to represent the needs of any and all residents to the institutional staff. Such a program makes the assumption that when a child is institutionalized and labeled by various public agencies as deviant the child is in crisis with society and is in need of someone to intervene in his behalf. Children traditionally are to be "seen and not heard" unless they counter the "normal" expectations of society. By the time a child reaches any institution, his dignity, self-respect, and ego have taken a terrific battering. At this point, the institution often aids and abets this process of dehumanizing the individual. With such probabilities in mind, an in-house institutional advocacy program assumes that even though skills may be developed and treatment given to a prospective resident, institutions traditionally are not growth inducing places in which children should be.

An in-house institutional advocacy program must oftentimes, with few resources and little acceptance, be willing to pursue the rights of residents through whatever appropriate means necessary. This process could range from obtaining socks for the sockless to representing residents in criminal court (as a friend of the court) on charges of rape, assault, or breaking and entering. For example, the advocacy program is unique in that it takes a positive but critical look at the services of an institution and negotiates for change. Obviously, such an approach is generally unpopular. Initially and on many occasions thereafter, such an advocacy program is seen as a threat by even well-meaning staff, while to the resident and others it appears as a supporting agent for the residents themselves.

The in-house system of advocacy may also be seen as an instrument of change. In ways, this change represents a social movement bringing to light prejudices and in some cases the denial of the most basic rights of handicapped children in both institutions and communities. The old saying that "everyone loves children" apparently has excluded handicapped or deviant children. Advocacy is an instrument to change this attitude. As the institutional care of human beings lumbers through the twentieth century, advocacy could be leading the charge. Advocacy views as potentially dangerous any system, agency, or parent who attempts to label children. Institutions may be looked upon as places society has created to hide children or adults who are not acceptable to the cultural norm, much like the segregation of blacks and the Indians in the past. Laws have been written supposedly to protect them, but these laws are oftentimes used against them. Public agencies have been created to represent the handicapped, but they more often than not turn out to be a mechanism for removing the handicapped from society. Advocacy, particularly in an institution, brings the inequality and bigotry of human services to light and exposes the potential dangers of institutions.

If given the chance and with proper commitment, advocacy can change human services to meet needs rather than to create needs. Obviously, there would be no need for advocacy if human needs were being met appropriately and decently.

WHY?

Since the beginning of time, society has sequestered people deemed deviant. As if to assuage its conscience, there have been, over the ages, episodic attempts at reformation. The fires of reformation have flickered and gone out only to be rekindled by guilt. Few mechanisms have evolved through which constructive help could be offered to those who have been labeled deviant. Advocacy can be the catalyst for a lasting and productive reformation.

In the past few decades, mechanisms have been developed which could have provided some of the answer—"circle of services," "the client centered approach," "normalization," "deinstitutionalization," and "institutional reform," to list only a few.

As early as 1906, P. L. Murphy reported success in taking mentally handicapped people out of a large institutional setting and putting them into small "colony" buildings where family-style living seemed to provide the warmth and society that was missing in the large wards of the institution. Murphy described improvement in people through what he believed to be a more normalized milieu. Unfortunately, the colonies were later abandoned and the institutions simply made larger. Dr. Murphy's attempt at reformation was short-lived. With the recent evolution of the geographic unit system in large mental hospitals, and with the development of group homes, we have come full circle back to Murphy's ideas.

If one looks closely at the tiny blips on the "polygraph" of reformation, it can be ascertained that, even in these minor excursions, there follows almost immediate drift away from meeting the needs of the most handicapped toward working with those who are less handicapped. There has been no force consistently present to maintain the focus of reform as it relates to those whose needs are the most difficult to meet. Advocacy, when properly supported and given the freedom and protection required, can be the means of maintaining this interest. If necessary, it can be the irritant that will promote in society something more than a rash of reform amounting to something more than a "seven year itch."

Those who have worked closely with people whose needs and handicaps are the greatest and most complex know that communicating such needs can be frustrating. The translation and amplification of cries for help and demands for attention require a sensitivity that can perceive the most subtle signal. Advocacy, when properly equipped, can receive and react to those outcries, thus bringing attention to them for remediation.

Even the most dedicated and motivated providers of service can become acclimated and even regimented in such ways as to participate in the drift theory (moving from working with the more handicapped to lesser handicapped) mentioned above. An advocate, unencumbered by service commitments and program quotas, can constantly call attention to the results of regimentation and institutionalization that occur even in the best of circumstances. Full-time advocates, uncommitted to direct service, can be certain that, in the zest to make all people like ourselves, those of us who make up the system are not simply fulfilling our own unmet needs. The advocate, whose responsibility does not include the direct provision of service, is better able to remain objective in establishing priorities and selecting needs that demand and require fulfillment in handicapped people.

In order to blur the lines or barriers that have separated the institutions from the communities, people are needed who can see that relationship from a vantage point. Such a position can only be maintained by persons who are not involved in the provision of direct service. The advocates in institutions can join advocates in communities to facilitate the true development of a circle of services to the advantage of handicapped people who, too often, find themselves caught in the large chasm that exists between communities and institutions. In these times of standardization and regimentation, there is always the chance that standards may reflect society's needs and not the needs of those for whom the service is intended. Advocates, who are without service commitments, may better see things as they truly are and can thus most appropriately and constructively criticize the developing standards which today represent the organization and limitations of society's collective conscience.

In the lives of all those whose "deviancy" is well hidden or tolerated and who are, consequently, referred to as "normal," there is usually awareness of the various rights that have been guaranteed by the United States Constitution. Children who can and do attend Sunday school, kindergarten, public schools, and the like, are continually exposed to their rights and responsibilities of citizenship, or at least to the rights they may expect on reaching the age of majority. It is interesting to note in reference to majority a recent utterance by Judge Blackmun of the United States Supreme Court, "Constitutional rights do not mature and come into being magically only when one attains the State-defined age of majority." For the most part, people with special needs—needs that began early in life—have never been told they have rights at all. They have never sung the songs of patriotism and have never been told the glowing history of these rights. They have never heard of counselors or attorneys and, if they had, they would not know how to find one of their own. For the most part, the severely handicapped do not even recognize the functional absence of citizenship.

Advocates, with broader knowledge of contemporary litigation, could bring the citizen who is severely or profoundly handicapped into a position where his or her needs could be heard, adjudicated, and met. Recently, a full-time advocate in one institution was explaining to a young man his rights of citizenship. When she finished the explanation, she asked if the young man had any questions, and he said: "Does the staff know about this yet?"

Full-time advocates are needed within institutions so the machinery of bureaucracy can constantly be inspected to see that it presents requests and priorities that reflect the true needs of those who are without their natural advocates or who, for reason of handicap or special needs, cannot speak for themselves. Advocates must be present among even the best intentioned in order to insure that their enthusiasm is related to the needs as handicapped children and people perceive them. Advocates are also necessary to reinforce the good things that may be happening to and for handicapped people.

WHY NOT?

It is interesting that, of the many reformations in which institutions have been involved over the years, none have had advocacy as a basic ingredient. It is remarkable that such a necessary and effective monitoring device has never been included in the desire to bring decency to the lives of those institutionalized. If not conscience, it would seem that even economy might have earlier dictated it to be so. In this country, where the needs of children and the handicapped have so long been heralded as a major commitment, the absence of advocacy is striking. This absence makes one wonder why. Adams and McDonald (1968), in "Clinical Cooling Out of Poor People," offer an opinion. They describe a process developed by professionals that is used to avoid direct and meaningful contact with people, a process they refer to as "cooling out." They demonstrate the many subtle and not-so-subtle mechanisms whereby such people are denied the receipt of service. One example given is the advertisement of services in conjunction with the development of waiting lists. Typically, agencies and institutions promote their ability to provide service, only to have the would be recipients who take the bait to find on arrival that long waiting lists have accumulated. Why advocacy? The presence of advocacy tends to expose "cooling out," thus making professional people more susceptible to direct contact with those they serve.

The ego thrust being made by many service systems to educate all those around them to give direct services is oftentimes simply another method of "cooling out" people who are in need to direct service. As long as the would be service providers are lecturing all those around them on how to meet special needs, they themselves do not become encumbered by the challenge of working with multiply handicapped people.

Why advocacy? Advocacy tends to remove the shroud of mystery that is oftentimes created and nurtured unknowingly by professionals as they constantly are engaged in agency territoriality. Even though an agency may cry out for additional staff, it will cry even louder if some of its service catchment area is about to be taken from it by a similar or competing agency.

Why not full-time advocacy? When one is introduced to a full-time advocate, the thought may occur, "If the person is an advocate, then what am I?" Is it the fear that others can do the job better or that a person's shortcomings will be exposed that so sensitizes some people on meeting a full-time advocate?

Who speaks for children? Who speaks for handicapped adults? How often have we considered what they would say if they could speak for themselves? Advocates "turn up the volume" until the sound is not only heard, but until its reverberations are felt. Perhaps these very sounds give answer to the question, "Why not?"

Why not full-time advocates in institutions? Their presence in institutions will insure that the traditional equilibrium that is rapidly established between those who serve and those who are to be served will be constantly kept off balance. It is easy to rationalize external criticism, but quite another thing to grapple with constructive criticism from within. Advocacy, by its very nature, is disruptive of regimentation. It constantly calls attention to the many subtleties of institutionalization, to the nature of restrictive environments, and to the lack of imagination in programming.

Why not advocacy? Advocacy is oftentimes in conflict with the family-centered approach. Too often, that approach simply means that whatever decision reached by the group of adults is what will be done with and for the handicapped child. At times, it may seem that advocates place in opposition the rights and needs of the child and the wishes and interests of parents or parent surrogates. Advocacy demands that participatory management include the participants in programming—that is, handicapped people themselves. Advocacy demands that various systems approaches be examined and held accountable for a humanitarian approach to handicapped people. Advocacy, in contrast to an adversary position, requires the reinforcement of good behavior on the part of the service-delivery staff.

The practice of meaningful advocacy can be a lonely job. Popularity ratings among the staff may be low, and crowds of supporters will thin as tradition is challenged. The energy consumed and expended in

such endeavors is often great. The rewards and successes may be slow
in coming. On the other hand, the negative reinforcers are sudden. It is
difficult work.

WHEN?

The advocate's first responsibility is to initiate and maintain a close personal relationship with those residents to whom he or she is responsible.
The advocate must be aware of a resident's individual needs, as seen by
the resident himself and of how the resident sees himself with regard to
his stay in the institution. The relationship between the resident and his
or her family, cottage parents, and teacher is of primary importance to
the advocate simply because it is of primary importance to the resident.
At any point that the resident feels in conflict with or in jeopardy from
whatever system supposedly has his or her care, it becomes the advocate's issue and calls for intervention. The advocate must be sensitive to
small needs as well as large needs, as expressed by the individual resident, and respond to both from the resident's perspective. There are
children in institutions who seem to be perpetually in conflict with the
institution, and it is with these that the advocate spends the majority of
his or her time. The role of "crisis" intervention is perhaps at the basis
of an in-house advocacy program. Far too often, residents of institutions are labeled "behavior problems"; and, because of their inability to
verbalize their needs at a professional level, staff are either unable to
comprehend or are unwilling to bend their professional standards to
meet these needs. An in-house advocate serves as an interpreter to professionals in order to explain the residents' needs. It is a relatively new
experience that professionals and human services are cognizant of the
needs of whom they serve rather than determining these needs by re-
membering Social Studies 101 in college. Institutions traditionally seem
to aim toward perpetuating the institution rather than serving the residents, and this also calls for advocate intervention. Far too often, the
grass is mowed for the esthetic value to the community rather than to
provide more playground room for the resident. An advocate must be
prepared to provide a different perspective to those in administration
who tend to see the residents as statistics and patients rather than human beings, who, because of their presence in an institution, have a
problem.

Institutions, because of the nature of the beast, tend to refuse services to residents who refuse to cooperate with those services. Although

this lack of cooperation is an indication of the residents' needs, it is common that when these services are refused this denial compounds the residents' problem and therefore becomes an advocacy issue. This could also be interpreted as a lack of professional ethics. It is also an advocacy view that when professionals state they cannot understand residents' point of view it is either a transference of responsibility or a lack of willingness to serve.

The process of setting priorities that institutions regularly undertake of how best to serve is often a subtle means of "cooling out" those problems institutions may be aware of, but are incapable of or unwilling to solve. Advocates assume that somewhere in the mass of bureaucratic jungle there is someone responsible for providing any service a resident has a need of. Advocates must be wary for the attitude of any professional system of service delivery to residents, for occasionally professional concerns adjust the resident to the system and not the system to the resident. The best example of this is institutions with priorities on research and with their higher-paid staff in research and lesser emphasis on direct services to residents. When an institution builds buildings and does not provide good direct service, it is poor priority selection.

In-house advocates ideally work in conjunction with anyone who has responsibilities to any given resident. The process of identifying an advocate is not a difficult one, and liaison can then be established to aid in the process of advocating for residents. More often than not the residents themselves will identify to the professional advocate those staff members to whom the resident feels allied. An advocate then builds and maintains a strong and positive relationship with these staff members which provides a great source of information about the residents and their needs.

WITH WHOM?

The task of identifying residents in need of an advocate's intervention is perhaps the simplest of an advocate's responsibilities. Those residents are often in a crisis within the institution, and advocates, through necessity, tend to deal more with them than with the resident who is maintaining the status quo. It is true that the higher functioning the resident, the more likely the resident is to be in conflict with the facility. This obviously speaks to the shortcomings of the facility and to inappropriate admissions, therefore necessitating advocacy.

Advocates hear the common phrases around an institution of "acting out," "behavior problem" residents. This obviously takes many and varying forms, but it means the resident is not adapting to the institution. The advocacy role, therefore, would be to adapt the institution to the resident. The irony, of course, in this labeling process of institutionalized children is that this same process is very likely what led the resident to be institutionalized, whether by public school, parents, or other human-service agencies in the community. Once a resident in crisis has been identified, the process of moving to see that the resident's needs are met is the advocate's responsibility.

Advocates traditionally deal with the top 10 percent or the bottom 10 percent of residents at an institution. Like public school or other public agencies, the system is set up to meet the needs of the "great majority." The great majority could be defined as the residents who have become complacent and who have succumbed to institutionalization, or are so seriously handicapped as to eliminate any self-expression of need. Residents who do fight the system or rebel against institutionalization receive the bulk of programming, not so much to help the resident as to control and, therefore, maintain the status quo of the institution. The result is advocates spending a majority of their time with 20 percent and too little time with 80 percent of the residents. This obviously calls for more advocates to meet the needs of all residents in an institution.

When speaking for a resident in crisis it is important for an advocate to follow through to successful closure if he or she is to maintain credibility with residents and staff. From a resident's perspective the follow-through to closure distinguishes between other professional services and advocacy.

HOW?

The process or procedure of advocacy takes many different forms. The first and more obvious form, the mere presence of an advocate, sometimes improves treatment and programming. This should not be interpreted as intimidation, but rather by his or her presence an advocate is a reminder of resident rights. The second more likely form of advocacy is either accompanying a resident or taking his specific requests to the institutional staff and negotiating for change directly with those responsible. This is often just interpreting to the professionals what the resident is saying.

The advocate sits in on all treatment team rounds and any meetings regarding a resident. Too often programs are harsh and punitive in their attempts to treat a resident. In situations like this an advocate must use his or her "instruments" in order to ensure the resident's rights are not jeopardized. These instruments are state statutes on patient care, institutional accreditation standards, ICF standards, and resident rights policies which have been established by advocacy within the institution. As an example, if the treatment team feels that a resident's contact through telephone or mail should be stopped, an advocate may object and use state statutes on patient care, and federal law for that matter, to prevent this occurrence. Using these instruments an advocate may keep in front of the team the image of residents as human beings with desires and wants not unlike those fortunate enough to be in the community.

The most commonly used form of advocacy is one of negotiation. This negotiation consists of conferring with staff about residents' needs and working on alternatives of how to meet these needs. This breaks the old institutional philosophy of one way to treat a resident and, obviously, broadens the institution's self-delivery system. Typically, this process begins with those directly responsible for the residents' treatment and moves up the chain of command. For instance, an advocate would begin with the cottage parent responsible for implementing a program and negotiating with the resident's cottage parent and, if not satisfied with the negotiations, go to the cottage parent's supervisor, and from there to the unit director responsible for the cottage. If the advocate is still not satisfied, he or she has the option of going to the facility human rights committee. If an advocate does not reach adequate solution in the resident's or the advocate's opinion, the advocate moves into phase two. This phase is referred to as confrontation. This takes the form of laying down hard requests as opposed to soft requests in the negotiation phase and is more difficult for institutional staff to deal with. If adequate solution is not reached in this phase an advocate may opt to utilize whatever clout he has through the director's office or the Human Rights Advocacy Committee, using them as instruments of solution.

SO WHAT?

The practice of full-time advocacy within an institution, over a period of time, will result in many changes. First of all, the staff must accept the fact that the advocates have come to stay and are a real and meaningful part of the institution. The very best that can happen is that staff members themselves begin to realize their potential as natural advocates. Staff will again appreciate the feeling that comes from meeting the needs of a person and, better still, the rewards of helping a person to meet these needs him or herself. Experience demonstrates that once advocacy is accepted within an institution, other staff members are more secure in advocating for the basic needs and rights of the consumers. Therefore, the advocates are eventually joined by others who are at least willing to tolerate them and even to call upon them and seek their advice. Particularly on occasions when staff are confronted with quasi-legal situations such as permission for special procedures and discharges, they will themselves call upon the advocates to double check that the handicapped person's rights are being properly protected. The spontaneous request for help from other staff is thus seen coming first in the area of legal concern. Following closely upon this are the spontaneous requests by the staff for the advocates' input relative to the rights of the residents versus those of his or her parent or guardian as this relates to discharges or change in direction of programs. Thus many of the nuances of institutionalization can be rapidly challenged and reexamined.

Many service systems are fortunately disrupted, which affords the opportunity for replacing them. More importantly, the residents of the institution become aware that there is additional hope, that their concerns do count, and that their voices are heard, even when critical of the services being delivered to them. The value of parent participation can be seen as developing parents of institutional children into true advocates for their child and can be readily stimulated as a side effect of advocacy. After an initial period of hesitancy and doubt, advocates will be aided by the staff in decision-making. What were once looked upon to be cold and indifferent standards can be given new life and meaning from the standpoint of advocacy.

Advocacy can give the various review committees and human rights committees now being established in institutions proper liaison with residents and can translate from them meanings of various institutional processes. The inclusion of full-time advocates on such committees can also greatly strengthen these committees objectively. Residents of the institution become more likely to advocate effectively for themselves, having had the pattern set by the full-time advocates. Deinstitutionalization and quality control of service delivery systems within an institution become more personalized in the presence of advocacy. Advocacy, when properly functioning, also serves to attract well-qualified staff to the facility because advocacy implies openness of the environment.

WHERE TO?

With the thrust of deinstitutionalization, normalization, and institutional reform, changes will be occurring over the years in residential care facilities. In contrast to what many are proclaiming, these facilities will probably not disappear soon. Society demands the presence of these facilities and there is little that would indicate the direction will be otherwise. The institutions in the future can be different, and advocacy could make that difference a reality. In the future institutions will be small and serve only people who are multiply and profoundly handicapped. Stays in these institutions will be more of the nature of respite care, and institutions then become therapeutic detours and not dead-end streets.

Advocacy, given proper support and understanding, can help accomplish these changes by helping staff to constantly see that this direction is dictated by the needs of the residents and not of the system itself. Advocacy can assure that parents eventually become trained to meet the needs of their children in such a way to make institutional care either unnecessary or transient in nature.

Perhaps the most challenging goal on the horizon of institutional care for those advocates so involved is the challenge to have deviancy accepted. Inherent in the label "deviant" is the assumption that those who are so labeled are basically quite different from the rest of us. The right to be different will, perhaps, be the last of the fundamental rights to be accepted by society.

REFERENCES

Adams, Paul L., and McDonald, Nancy S. "Clinical Cooling Out of Poor People." *American Journal of Orthopsychiatry,* 38 (April, 1968).

Murphy, P. L. "Colony Treatment of the Insane and Other Defectives" *Carolina Medical Journal* (June, 1906).

7

Child Advocacy in Government:
A Statewide Program

JOHN W. PELOSI
DONALD TAYLOR
JAMES L. PAUL

N ORTH CAROLINA was among the first states to develop and implement a legislatively mandated advocacy system within state government. This within-system advocacy arrangement provided the basis
for developing several major concepts of advocacy and for further examining the proposition that advocacy can work inside the system.

This chapter will (1) describe some of the issues and basic concepts of advocacy articulated in the state child advocacy program, and
(2) describe certain aspects of the practice of advocacy in terms of the
advocacy process as it is manifested in the work of the field staff in the
advocacy program.

One of the first issues to be faced in the program is the definition
of advocacy. A definition that is so vague as to not suggest any specific
activity is not likely to receive support. A limiting definition, on the
other hand, that constrains legitimate advocacy activity is ultimately
defeating. Advocacy is defined in different ways within the state structure, usually depending on the particular job to be done by the person
doing the defining. A secretary of a human resource department is likely
to be interested in child advocacy as a way to determine needs of children across the usual categorical and agency boundaries and to develop
priorities for services. A legislator may see advocacy as a way to coordi-

nate the different programs for children within the service delivery network. An agency director may see advocacy as a means for increasing resources for children's services. Consumer organizations are more likely to highlight the monitoring functions in their view of advocacy.

All of these are indeed important aspects of advocacy. A major feature in insuring the success of an advocacy program within state government is the orchestration of various legitimate advocacy interests so that human services become responsive and accountable to children. Any child advocacy program within state government must be sensitive to the expectancies of citizens, policy-makers, and service providers. Conflicting expectancies can result in the assumption of conflicting roles that confuse both staff and clients. Resolving these conflicting expectancies results in broadening the constituency for advocacy support. This is a necessary condition for the survival of advocacy within the system.

The organizational position of the advocacy structure within the state system is important. It must be accorded the administrative authority to implement its legislated responsibilities. Yet it must "fit" as part of the system it seeks to improve. This is a difficult political as well as organizational balance to obtain. The position must include sufficient bureaucratic autonomy to make possible the maintenance of an advocacy rather than a service delivery perspective. Yet it must be close enough to the policy-formulating and decision-making structure to make advocacy work as a predominantly persuasive, information-based, client-feedback process for change. The more remote system for change is likely to be more adversarial, more confrontation oriented, and more legalistic. The dynamics of change in these two situations are very different.

The bureaucratic characteristics of child-serving systems create many problems in the delivery of quality services to children. These include, for example, difficulties in responding quickly and effectively to the service needs of children and the tendency to not coordinate service efforts with other potential child and family resources. Advocacy within the system can monitor, shape, and maintain the bureaucratic improvement over time.

The advocacy system is drawn naturally into a bureaucratic identity. Some of this is an inevitable cost of the within-system effort and is not altogether undesirable. Sometimes the child's advocacy interest is best served by the advocate's identification with the system itself. Easy access to information and facilitating entry into some situations would be examples.

Advocacy must, however, avoid the co-optation and total control by the bureaucracy it seeks to change on behalf of children. *Bureaucratic anomie is the Achilles' heel of within-systems advocacy.* This is frequently avoided as much by the diplomacy of advocates as by organizational assurances.

There are several strategies vital to the effective functioning of advocacy within the system that facilitate the identity and development of the advocacy mission. These approach the status of principles in the North Carolina experience of developing advocacy within the state system. They are outlined below as important conditions for advocacy within the system.

1. Maintain a close alliance with a constituency outside the governmental jurisdiction.
2. Raise the advocacy consciousness of workers in the child service system and promoting their advocacy potential.
3. Reserve the right to go to the source of power in government when negotiations fail.
4. Maintain linkages with those parts of the political system that appropriate resources and set policies.

This is certainly not a complete list, but it does include some of the major themes emerging from our experiences.

There are currently four programs conducted by the North Carolina Child Advocacy Council. They include: (1) assistance to state departments and agencies in improving and coordinating their services; (2) assistance to citizens' and consumer groups; (3) direct advocacy for children, youth, and their families; and (4) initiating and/or supporting legislation responsive to the needs of children.

What has been described here is the broad program structure and philosophical perspective that has guided and is now manifested in the state child advocacy program in North Carolina. The advocates, or field staff, of the advocacy program have responsibility for making the direct-case advocacy aspect of the program work. It is their work in responding to individual child advocacy needs in local communities and regions that provides much of the substance and data basis for the advocacy work that goes on with state agencies and the legislature. The remaining portion of this chapter will describe principles of the field-based advocacy process.

PRINCIPLES OF THE FIELD-BASED ADVOCACY PROCESS

The field staff of the child advocacy program has responsibility for the development of and action taken in agency coordination, direct case advocacy, class advocacy, development of advocacy systems, needs assessment, and resource and program development. Each staff member has three major functions:

A. Coordination of services and programs directed toward children and youth in county and multi-county departments and agencies in such a way that programs administered by different agencies designed to serve the same client population are integrated and complementary rather than duplicative. To accomplish this responsibility the Office for Children Field Consultant, within and between the counties in his multi-county area,

1. cooperates with respective local agency staff in periodic review of program planning;
2. reports to the Office for Children Regional Director the findings and implications of reviews relevant to regional planning;
3. submits to the Regional Director recommendations of action based on local needs assessment information;
4. assists in the review of the policies and regulations promulgated by appropriate local government and agencies which apply to eligibility for participation in programs and the general conduct of programs;
5. makes recommendations to local departments and agencies operating in counties and multi-counties concerning the improvement, expansion, deletion, or innovation of programs and services within the purview of the respective agency or department;
6. consults with appropriate staff of local departments and agencies on the design, organization, and staffing of programs and services for the purpose of improving, joining, and coordinating service delivery to children and their families;
7. calls and convenes conferences between and among various agencies, as the field consultant deems appropriate to the issue(s) relative to the integration of similar services and to the restructuring of services which are overlapping rather than complementary;
8. periodically meets and consults with local representatives and/or officers of consumer and professional organizations in order to actively involve them in local planning for children and youth;
9. participates in reviews of all new programs affecting children and youth proposed by any local agency or department;

10. assists in dissemination of information concerning legislation and funding sources related to services for children and youth to consumers, private citizens, and public officials.

B. Promotion of increased awareness of and responsiveness to the rights and needs of both individual children, youth, their parents, and guardians on the part of county and multi-county and other public agencies. To accomplish this responsibility the Office for Children Field Consultant

1. conducts a direct case advocacy function to insure that local agencies respond to the needs of children and their families. The consultant performs this function by
   a. investigating individual cases;
   b. assessing individual cases;
   c. appropriately intervening or responding; and
   d. recording and documenting activity on each case brought to his attention.
2. develops local advocacy systems, involving local consumers, providers of services, and other community leaders; maintains liaison with and provides technical assistance to local child advocacy systems;
3. meets with county and multi-county directors or officers of consumer and professional organizations for the purpose of informing them about local issues related to children and promoting joint planning to fill the gaps in services;
4. organizes and/or participates in conferences for professionals, consumers, and other interested citizenry related to the philosophy, conceptualization, and implementation of programs and services for children and youth at the county and multi-county levels;
5. organizes and conducts local and area workshops of consumer and agency groups for the purpose of developing new programs and improvement of existing programs for children and youth;
6. takes part in planning and implementation of an active public awareness effort concerning children and youth, utilizing news media and public presentations at the county and multi-county level.

C. Management of Office for Children Findings at the county and multi-county level

1. prepares reports to carry out directives requested by the Regional Director relevant to regional and local planning;

2. documents actual deficiencies in service delivery systems at the local level resulting from local departments and agency policies and procedures, state and agency policies and procedures, lack of local resources, and the need for legislative deletions, amendments, or new action based on children's needs at the local level;
3. documents and maintains confidential files on individual advocacy cases;
4. maintains continuing needs assessment for children and youth in the local communities.

The overall field-based advocacy process is carried out within these three functions. It is important to recognize that the balance between these three functions must be managed with care. It is relatively easy for one function to dominate the others. It is also possible that the functions can conflict with each other, thereby causing dissonance in the child-service network, as well as in the field staff person.

One way to discuss how the field-based advocacy process works is to focus on one of the functions and show its relationship to the others. The function closest to the generic definition of child advocacy is the second function, which includes both direct case advocacy and developing local advocacy systems, as well as other activities important to this function. Here, the focus will be on the direct case advocacy function.

Field staff, or field consultants, as they are called, can become involved in direct case advocacy by referral from a person at the local level—a parent or a professional working closely with a child—who sees a problem that cannot be easily solved, or by way of the hotline (a toll free telephone line operated by the Department of Human Resources, available to all citizens having concerns about the delivery of services).

Direct case advocacy can involve an individual child and the family in a situation already highly charged with problems. The problems may concern attempts to obtain services from one or more agencies. The field consultant must also work within a spirit of communication, cooperation, and collaboration.

The first step of the field consultant should always be to carefully investigate the situation. It is possible to assume that the referral information is accurate while proceeding to collect additional data about the issues and problems involved. A relatively complete picture of the situation must be obtained before attempting to assess it and designing a plan to correct it.

The role of field consultant itself provides a natural context in which to begin each case in a spirit of thoughtful questioning. Field consultants have contacts with many people serving at different levels and many different agencies in the service network. The role of coordinator provides the field consultant with a natural entry into various parts of the service system.

A number of advocacy situations can be handled because of the field consultant's comprehensive knowledge of the service network at the local level. The service system has become more and more complex. Parents occasionally get the impression that an agency should be providing a service to their child which the agency is in fact not legally mandated to provide. The case advocacy function of the field consultant puts him or her in an extremely useful position to facilitate communication between consumers and agencies and to head off some problems before they get out of proportion.

Obviously, there are instances in which direct case advocacy is needed but where the problem is not communicative. For example, if a child needs service, but no service is delivered, it could be that the needed service is simply not available in the community. Or, though available, it is full to capacity. Another possibility is that the service is available but the child's parents or other natural advocates do not know how to bring the child to the service. A fourth possibility is that the needed service is available, but the agency rejects the child for some less than valid reason.

All of the above situations are characterized by a child's needing service but the service is not available to the child. There are other types of situations. One is that a child receives inadequate service, as judged by reasonable standards. Another is that a child receives inappropriate service—a service that is not needed—and thus the child is being over-served.

A final type of situation mentioned here is very important. It occurs when a child is receiving a particular service, but one or more of the people close to the child do not like the way the service is being delivered. Or they may not like the service itself or certain aspects of the delivery process, even though it is clearly legal. One example of this type of situation involves public schools. It is a law in North Carolina that children may be paddled by school personnel. Many people, both parents and school personnel, support the law, while many are working to change it.

The point here is that even though paddling is sanctioned by law, the situation is not clear cut, because those who oppose this law have different values about children and how to treat them. Many advocacy situations are not clear cut. Rather than violation of some legal right or entitlement for service, rather than negligence or incompetence on the part of service deliverers, rather than some service being unavailable to a child because the service does not exist, the problem may be a difference in values between two different groups of people.

This list of possibilities of breakdown in services is not meant to be exhaustive. It hints at the complexity of the field-based advocacy program:

1. There are many different types of advocacy situations and they call for different strategies, different actions; it is very important to recognize that and to analyze each case on its individual circumstances.

2. It may be very useful to develop decision rules for case selection. It may be that there are some cases that should not be handled or that *cannot* be handled for various reasons. The necessity for decision guidelines increases if the number of direct advocacy cases increases and program resources do not increase. Decision guidelines for case selection may vary depending upon program resources and mandates. Local advocacy groups have an important role to play in advocacy cases involving value differences. It may be very useful to construct some kind of screening instrument to help determine the extent to which value differences are involved. These cases can be among the toughest, and if attempts are not made to understand the importance of value differences, some advocacy situations will not only be confusing, they may be explosive as well.

3. Another point is that most of the different types listed do not involve incompetence or negligence on the part of an agency or a person in an agency. Many can involve some kind of breakdown in the service network, rather than in some particular service agency, which is where another function of the field consultant comes in. It is the "needs assessment" function in which gaps and cracks in the system are discovered. The direct case advocacy function adds a needed dimension to the other functions of coordination and needs assessment.

The direct case advocacy function allows field consultants to acquire a kind of information that is difficult to have—information about what is actually happening where service counts, directly with the client.

The three main functions of the field-based advocacy process fit together conceptually, if viewed in this way and if care is given to program management. Field consultants must have sufficient resources. They must also have a certain philosophical orientation which serves as a guide to their activities. One of the values underpinning this philosophy is the belief in the idea that it is not only all right to gently look over someone's shoulder at his work, but that it is a powerful advocacy tool. In cases where a staff person may have allowed his professional skill to slip momentarily, this approach may solve a problem quickly and easily, without forcing the staff person to defend his professional honor.

Belief that the vast majority of people in the human services are in them because they want to help people, not to damage them, is also important. It is not easy to *never* make a mistake. It is easy to get sloppy when rushed, working with limited resources, *and* no one is watching.

Looking *gently* over someone's shoulder helps him to slow down and think about what is being looked at and what he is doing.

Some field consultants have established a step-by-step process in which they first go to the person who seems to be at the source of the advocacy concern.

Going directly to the source can frequently solve the problem. If that does not work, the advocate goes up the administration line to see the source's supervisor. If that does not work, advocates go the next step up. By making this step-by-step process explicit and open to all, several things operate to promote chances of success. First, there is a much greater chance to change a course of action in a neutral situation than in one where someone is backed against a wall defending his professional honor. Secondly, starting at the source and working step-by-step upward in the administration provides a better chance of protecting everyone's *interest*. Also, by starting at the source the field consultant is in the best position to collect direct information about the situation. Finally, this process tends to put the consultant in a position of negotiation rather than confrontation.

In summary, it is important to maintain a balance between a direct advocacy and the other functions. The role of coordinator-collaborator-facilitator for service network helps to head off the need for direct advocacy. Field consultants, by maintaining a helping, influencing role with respect to building a better service system, put themselves in a better position of effectiveness when the need arises for direct advocacy.

8

Advocacy Training

G. RONALD NEUFELD
JAMES L. PAUL

THIS CHAPTER PROVIDES an overview of training for advocates who are already engaged in some form of advocacy activity. It also suggests a role for universities and colleges in advocacy training. The philosophical orientation, while consistent with the within-system, or internal, advocacy view presented in other chapters, is expanded here to include citizen advocacy. The purpose of including this view of advocacy here is to provide an additional conceptual basis for examining advocacy training and presenting a more comprehensive view of the area. While not reviewed here, there have indeed been considerable efforts in the training of citizen advocates and the training of consumers for self advocacy. Advocacy training in these areas has been more thoroughly developed than specific training for internal advocacy.

There is no reason why training in these two domains, internal and external, should be mutually exclusive. While there are some fundamental differences in advocacy inside and outside the system, as will be discussed more fully here, it is to the reciprocal advantage of advocates inside and outside the service delivery system and to the client to build alliances that are mutually supportive, effective, and efficient.

If advocacy is to work it must proceed from a position of strength, and that means a competent advocate. A competent advocate must know how to advocate, when, with whom, and—sometimes it is not as obvious as it appears—for whom. Effective advocacy, as Paul points out in Chapter 2, must take into account the advocate's own personal needs as well as his technical resources. The advocate does not work in a vacuum, either personally or organizationally. He has his own community and must have his own resources for renewal as well as for train-

112

ing. He works in relation to organizations where, if he is in the system, as Riddle and King point out in Chapter 6, accountability can become a problem. Being accountable to the client can become very difficult in situations where the advocate cannot shed his organizational accountability.

Survival in a system as an advocate while effectively representing the interests of others, diplomacy in a conflict of interests between client needs and system interests where the client's concerns are not compromised, and sensitivity to the system and personal aspects of the "ecology of the issue" involved—all are basic training and development concerns.

The role functions outlined by Pelosi, Taylor, and Paul in Chapter 7 are complex functions within a system. The advocate's role, as they point out, is not always viewed as helpful or "in the interest of the system." What does one do then? How does one adapt to the role conflict and the dissonance this can stimulate in one's work? How does one handle the backwaters of work conflict that can flood into one's personal life?

The dual advocacy model described by Pappanikou in Chapter 5 that combines omsbudsmen and adversarial functions presents yet another example where training must be carefully designed to meet the substantive training needs and be provided in a format that fits the advocacy situation. While not in the best long-term interest of advocacy, the advocate, or the client, there is a certain degree of closure and structure in drawing a clear line between us and them, the advocates and the rest. It is, indeed, difficult to avoid this trap. How does one know when it is necessary to draw such a line? How does one know when the line has been drawn only out of self-defense and potential friends on "the other side" have been alienated? The affective as well as the cognitive needs of advocates for skills and ongoing support must be met.

The bridge between the within and citizens' advocacy, or internal and external, is in some ways a corollary in the larger service delivery area to the dual advocacy proposed by Pappanikou for the schools.

The inside and outside views will be briefly reviewed here to provide a basis for more extensive examination of these training issues.

THE ACCOUNTABILITY PROBLEM IN HUMAN SERVICES

The growth and expansion of the human service system in America since the 1950s has been enormous. On the one hand the American system has developed some highly innovative and exemplary programs that have gained worldwide recognition. On the other hand, the vast majority of persons in this country needing service are unable to obtain the support they need and to effectively gain access to resources in the system. The problem is not just one of inadequate resources; it is also due to lack of a holistic view. Within the American system there is a great deal of variance in the theory and philosophy that is practiced in the delivery system. Lack of service coordination often results from competition and disagreement between professionals and between agencies. Additional problems stem from the size and complexity of the system. Huge bureaucracies have evolved with responsibility for managing and distributing resources and operating a variety of programs.

The bureaucracy may be compared to a huge onion. The peeling away of one layer of bureaucracy simply brings another layer to the surface. Levels of bureaucracy extend from local communities to regional structures within a state, to state organizations, to multi-state regional structures, and culminate in the massive federal bureaucracy in Washington. Vertical communication between layers is often limited and effective local input to decisions at the state level is usually difficult to accomplish.

Similarly, horizontal communication at the same levels of bureaucracy is weak, and agencies at the same level are likely to fight with each other. This lack of coordination and communication, and agency warfare, contribute to a dismal picture of inadequate human services for many citizens in this country. A system has been created that often hinders, rather than helps citizens access resources that they need and resources that rightfully belong to them.

The set of circumstances described above is bringing about an erosion of the credibility of public employees in the bureaucracy, professionals in the system, and many service providers. Consumers and citizens outside the human service network are becoming more and more dissatisfied with these conditions. This dissatisfaction is expressed in a number of ways. First, human-service agencies have become popular targets for the public media, which sometimes results in employee routes and administrative reorganization of programs. The courts have become involved in order to bring about program accountability. Legal procedures have resulted in many new laws to protect the human rights of persons who interact with human service programs.

Another procedure used by human service agencies to develop accounting for services provided and clients served is management by objectives. This technique proposes to control program activities through the development of very specific and measurable objectives.

Finally, there is a strong movement under way to develop program standards. These standards are aimed at establishing minimum conditions to which all programs must conform.

The use of mass communication, legal procedures, program planning, and the development of standards are techniques that are being used in an attempt to render human-service organizations more accountable to the public. While each is all important and necessary, none adequately protects individual clients in the system or individuals attempting to access the system.

ADVOCACY: AN INTEGRATIVE APPROACH

It is the recognition of the blurring of individual human rights and needs that has given rise in recent years to the human advocacy movement. Aimed at an individual and performed by an individual, advocacy is as old as the human race. Very simply, it takes the form of a concerned person acting in behalf of or pleading a cause for another individual.

Given the size, complexity, and impersonal nature of many of our human-service arrangements, it is often impossible for even competent and highly independent individuals to advocate for themselves. Competent individuals are often dominated by large organizations. Likewise, an individual advocate is likely to have limited success in advocating for a client in the system, unless the advocate knows the system and its resources or has access to political power. Information and power or access to power are prerequisite to influencing our systems.

Due to the apparent breakdown of the informal human advocacy procedures that have operated in the past in less complex environments, we are confronted by a need to develop some new advocacy approaches. Since the cornerstone of advocacy revolves around responsiveness to individual client needs, advocacy activity tends to resist structure and organization. However, because of the limited effectiveness of unstructured advocacy procedures from the past in the face of large inflexible organizations, it has become necessary to invest the concepts of advocacy with organization and structure. As a movement it could perhaps benefit from an examination of the procedures and structures associated with organizations that promote the civil rights and women's movements. Needed in advocacy is a movement aimed at assuring individual human rights, a movement aimed at rendering services accountable to their clients, a movement geared toward a functional yoking together of individual advocates, and a movement committed to identifying and providing support for effective advocates.

From the writers' viewpoint, the advocacy movement will be seriously limited unless it is successful in developing a collaborative bridge between advocates inside and outside the system. An integrative approach that makes use of the positive aspects of both internal advocacy and external advocacy has tactical and political as well as conceptual appeal. A fragmented, "magical solution" approach to problems of the magnitude and complexity of those involved in current human-service delivery systems is destined to failure. There are too few advocacy resources available to be able to afford fragmentation.

It is the purpose of the chapter to identify the rule of advocacy training both as a means of preparing advocates to effectively do their work, and the role of training in organizing advocates and motivating them for action. At this point advocacy training is very limited. Consumer organizations are providing some training in order to develop volunteer support in local communities for direct service. A few organizations have become involved in training related to legal advocacy, and a limited amount of advocacy training is provided in several universities. In general, training is limited and incomplete. Activities tend to take the form of short-term or single-event workshops, sponsored by small state or federal grants. Most advocates learn about advocacy and the human service system through trial and error. At best advocacy training is haphazard and limited, and much of the training that is presently provided presents advocacy as a system adversary approach. Due to the popular portrayal of advocacy as a system adversary mechanism, advocacy activity and the concept of advocacy is in constant jeopardy. If the concept of advocacy is going to survive, there will need to be an alliance between the public and the private sectors that supports advocacy activity. The advocacy movement both has and needs allies within the systems. However, the ability of advocacy activity in the system will always be limited apart from an alliance with advocates outside the system. Movement in the direction of an alliance between advocates from the public and the private sectors could be brought about through training.

This chapter examines the training arrangements that support different approaches to advocacy and suggests additional areas of training and training arrangements that are needed. Two major thrusts in advocacy are considered here to provide a comprehensive perspective on the issues involved in training. First, the concept of citizen or volunteer advocacy is examined. Second, the concept of internal advocacy within the system is reviewed for the purpose of focussing on training needs. Finally, a possible role in advocacy training is explored and recommended for universities. These training arrangements could be viewed as external advocacy training, in-service training, and pre-service training. It is the writers' belief that all advocacy training should have a strong experiential component closely linked to the service-delivery system.

VOLUNTEER OR CITIZEN ADVOCACY TRAINING

At this point in the evolution of advocacy activity in the United States the greatest support for advocacy has come from volunteers or citizens. One popular viewpoint is that only advocacy that is sponsored by and exercised from outside the human-service system is likely to be effective. The issues surrounding internal and external advocacy are examined below.

Internal advocates work within the systems that support them, whereas external advocates receive support from sources that are independent of the systems in which they perform their advocacy activities. One major objection to internal advocacy programs is that advocates in the system lose too much freedom to act in an objective, unbiased fashion in behalf of their clients—"whose bread I eat, his song I sing." To the extent that this adage is true, advocating within the system is a disadvantage. When client advocacy activity results in conflict between the advocate and the system providing his support, an advocate may feel pressured to compromise an ideal. It is difficult to bite a feeding hand. If a system resists the advocacy activity of the advocates it sponsors, it may employ a variety of "cooling out" tactics. For example, advocates may receive work assignments that create distance between them and their clients. The risk of system cooptation or "cooling out" suggests that there may be an advantage for providing independent support for the work of advocacy to give assurance that the system in which the advocates work will not control them.

One of the advantages of advocacy from within the system is that advocates are likely to have greater access to information about programs serving their clients. External advocates tend to be adversaries of the system. System adversaries are often disliked by service providers and they are therefore denied access to the service-delivery settings and to important sources of information. If advocates cannot monitor the delivery system directly, then the information on which they base their actions must be second-hand information. The actions and accusations of advocates must be based on accurate information. A rapid erosion of advocacy credibility will result from actions and accusations based on false information or incomplete data. System adversaries may be viewed as Quixotes tilting with windmills. They do not know the issues and they do not know the enemies.

Another important difference between internal and external advocacy concerns the tactics employed. Internal advocates are likely to believe that human-service systems can be renewed and that this renewal can be accomplished from within the system. When they are faced with a problem, their first approach is to bring about change by negotiation. Confrontation is a last resort.

It has already been pointed out that external advocates are often characterized by a strong negative system bias. They contend that our current human service systems are beyond redemption and must be dismantled. Their intent is to destroy and start anew. They view negotiation with the human service establishment as a waste of time and move immediately to confrontation. Caught up as they often are with their obsession to tear down the existing structures of the system, they sometimes overlook their advocacy goals and fail to foresee the injuries that their clients may suffer in the system dismantling process. Additionally, the external advocate may not be able to offer the support a client may need if existing services are withdrawn. They may see the problems, but stop short of providing solutions much like the terrier chasing a locomotive. What will he do with it when he catches it? There are many natural advocates and potential advocacy allies in the system. A wholesale condemnation of the system, all of its parts, and all its personnel, is likely to stand in the way of an alliance between the internal resources and an advocacy movement.

Another disadvantage of external advocacy programs is that they tend to be transient. Financial support is often small and short term. A single charismatic leader is often responsible for the genesis and direction of the program. Generally, a small band of highly committed persons work toward solving a small number of specific problems. When the problems are solved or appear insoluble, when financial support collapses, or when the leader disappears, the movement is likely to vanish.

This polarization of internal and external advocacy activity is seldom witnessed in the extreme forms described. However, the distinction between internal and external advocacy is a useful one in order to help advocates consider the relative strengths and weaknesses of the different approaches. Despite the differences between the internal and external advocacy approaches, it is likely that they would agree on the problems. The differences between the two approaches concern the tactics they use. Obviously there are advantages and disadvantages to both internal and external advocacy approaches. For advocacy to become an effective social movement, it will be necessary to integrate the strengths from both approaches.

At present advocacy training for citizens and volunteers tends to be conducted by consumer organizations such as state associations for retarded citizens, state cerebral palsy organizations, and societies for autistic children. Their training is aimed at preparing volunteers to provide case advocacy for individual clients. Many of these programs are valuable at the level of identifying friends for handicapped persons and for providing enrichment or social activities. There are two other areas of training that need to be made available to interested citizens from the private sector. First, training should be provided to strengthen the skills of citizens to lobby in behalf of handicapped citizens. Second, citizens from the private sector need training that enables them to function as board members and consultants to public programs and to regional, state, and federal agencies. This is necessary in order to redirect the accountability of the service-delivery system to the public and the clients rather than to the system itself.

The content of training for volunteers interested in providing direct service or being a case advocate would include the following: client communication, normalization principles, human and legal rights, monitoring procedures, system resources, techniques for data collection, and negotiation versus confrontation tactics. At this level of advocacy, an advocate should have the skills and interest in being a friend, companion, and counselor. Beyond that, an advocate should be willing to negotiate or fight for a client whose legal or human rights are in jeopardy or are being ignored. In this connection, training for advocates should include information concerning support structures for advocates. Advocates working in isolation are likely to become very discouraged if they are unable to generate support for their activities from the system. At that point both personal and organizational support are needed to help the advocate and client obtain their objectives.

Training for citizens and volunteers tends to take the form of an intensive workshop. This is unfortunate, from the writers' viewpoint. It is likely that the quality of volunteer activity would be greatly improved if training were continuous and took the form of short didactic sessions, allowing for a great deal of interaction between participants. This procedure would provide opportunities for advocates to talk with and support each other. Over time it is likely and desirable that a cohesive organization would emerge. This organization could help with needs assessments and to support lobbying activities at the state and federal levels.

Another level of advocacy focuses on persons with skills and interests in participating on a wide variety of boards. There is a growing trend to include consumers and citizens from the private sector to participate on boards at the local, state, and federal levels. Local programs and projects that provide direct service often establish boards with consumer representation. There are boards at the regional level within states and boards that operate at the state and federal levels. State agency employees and professionals often complain that these boards are a hindrance rather than a help in service provision. They criticize consumer members for complaining about conditions affecting one or two clients or that they have such limited information about programs and services that they are unable to contribute to board activity. In some instances, these complaints may be valid. In other instances the complaints may be valid. In other instances the complaints simply reflect resistance in the system to be accountable to the public and to consumers.

In any event, training is needed for persons who are interested in serving on such boards. In the writers' opinion it is important that such persons have some direct contact with individual clients that they would represent. It would be helpful for consumer or citizen board members to have intensive training aimed at case advocacy procedures. Beyond the above experience and training, a board member should be trained concerning client needs, service monitoring, system resources, decision-making procedures in the system, and negotiation-confrontation procedures.

Training should include the development of an information system that establishes communication between case advocates and board members at all levels. Effective participation on boards at the state and federal levels could be very helpful in creating an advocacy alliance between the public and the private sector and between agencies and consumer organizations.

IN-SERVICE TRAINING FOR ADVOCACY

Although consumer organizations have been active in training volunteer or citizen advocates, this activity has had little if any effect on the service-delivery system. It has already been stated that many people view effective advocacy as impossible from inside the system. At the same time external advocates have been likely to confront the system without having set in place mechanisms to influence constructive change.

Advocacy mechanisms are needed in the service delivery system for four reasons: (1) external advocates often lack access to information from the system, (2) there are often discrepancies between client needs and services, (3) clients may have difficulty gaining access to existing resources, and (4) the human or legal rights of advocates are often violated. There are many existing and potential advocates within the service-delivery system—persons who could render services much more responsive to client needs if training were available and if support could be secured from the private sector. But one might ask the question, what is the relationship between advocacy and responsibility? Is a teacher functioning as an advocate when performing well as a teacher? Is a cottage parent an advocate when that staff rule is being exercised?

An advocacy commitment embraces a willingness to move beyond the rule for which one is being paid when client welfare is at stake. For example, suppose that a math teacher discovers a student has visual difficulty and needs glasses. Furthermore, suppose that the student's family lacks resources to purchase glasses. The teacher is performing as an advocate when he or she moves beyond the teaching role to help the student obtain glasses. In a residential institution a recreation worker is paid to provide recreational training and enrichment to institution residents. If the employee in the recreation department observes that a certain resident comes to sessions every day with bruises, he would be functioning as an advocate if he undertook to identify the reason for the bruises and try to eliminate that cause.

It is clear that many of the weaknesses in our service-delivery system could be eliminated if staff in the system had a commitment to advocacy that extended beyond the role for which they were paid. Unfortunately our current training arrangements tend to reinforce single roles. Likewise there is a growing tendency for persons in our social system to avoid intervention in the lives of others. It is this detachment that enables a crowd to watch a woman get beaten and robbed in broad daylight in the heart of a city. An advocacy commitment opposes this kind of social detachment. An advocacy commitment encourages persons to extend themselves beyond their formal roles in an organization if that extension of roles is likely to improve the quality of life for a client or a friend.

In-service advocacy training within the service-delivery system should be designed to promote a dual role for employees. One writer participated in one experiment in which the dual role was promoted. The experiment was conducted in a residential institution for persons labeled retarded. To begin with, all staff that interacted with the residents were identified with the exception of housekeeping, maintenance, and dietary staff. The staff-to-resident ratio was 1:4. It was pointed out to staff members that many residents were not receiving the services they needed. The activities of residents throughout the 24-hour time frame of their day and the activities of residents between services and departments were not examined. Reviews of programs for residents were irregular and infrequent, and many residents lacked close contact with staff.

It was therefore proposed that all institution staff adopt no more than four clients for whom they would function as advocates. Hence, staff members in their formal roles may have been social workers, educators, or cottage parents. They would also now have an advocacy role. As an advocate, the staff member was encouraged to develop a close personal relationship to four residents. Residents in turn were encouraged to relate closely to their advocates. Staff advocates were expected to know more about their four advocate clients than anyone else in the client's life space. They were to know why the client was in the institution. They were to know what kind of a program was in place for the residents and what each resident was doing throughout the 24-hour period of the client's day. The advocate was expected to know whether or not a client's program was responsive to his needs. If a resident's needs were not being met or if his human or legal rights were being violated, the advocate was expected to negotiate for his client's needs. If negotiations broke down, the advocate was encouraged to immediately contact the superintendent or the Human Rights Committee.

Finally, on a monthly basis, the advocate was expected to justify the presence of the resident in the institution. If an advocate could not adequately do so, he was expected to participate in a plan to deinstitutionalize the resident.

Residents in the institution very quickly captured the concept of advocacy. It was observed that the residents would often compare notes on advocates at the level of what their advocate was doing for them. In this regard an advocacy program can serve as a staff-evaluation tool from a resident's perspective. It was also observed that some staff members were never able to function well in an advocacy role. It is the writers' view that staff who cannot function well as advocates should not be placed in a role of direct service provision in any human service system.

Finally, it was observed that the advocacy role in the institution served as a mechanism to bring about improved and more frequent vertical communication and interaction within the institution between lower- and upper-level staff in the institutional hierarchy.

Training and support are needed for dual advocacy roles as described above. The content of training would include an examination of the institution's resources, data collection procedures, training concerning communication with a resident's parents and natural community, training concerning the legal rights of residents, an examination of normalization concepts, and finally, negotiation procedures. Training should be ongoing and based on the assessed needs of each individual. Staff should then be encouraged to exercise the content of training with residents for whom they are advocates.

Certain training resources are usually available to agencies at the state level. This money is often distributed to state-supported programs for staff in-service training. Additional training money is also available from federal sources. In most instances it is likely that an agency would receive better training if it contracted with an external organization. Training procedures too closely related to the service-delivery system may have difficulty dealing with aspects of advocacy procedures that confront weakness within the organization. In order to create a necessary alliance, it would seem reasonable that state programs and volunteer organizations alike would benefit from some joint training arrangements.

ADVOCACY TRAINING: A ROLE FOR HIGHER EDUCATION

Previous sections of this chapter have focused on volunteer advocacy roles and a dual-advocacy–staff role of employees in the service-delivery system. A limited number of organizations have taken steps to hire full-time advocates. These organizations include residential institutions and state agencies. In some instances full-time advocates function as case advocates. A more productive role for full-time advocates is to function as ombudsmen. An advocate as ombudsman relates to specific advocacy cases and then moves toward identifying organizational staff or administrative shortcomings in the system that allowed the problem to occur. Obviously an advocate in an ombudsman role must have a great deal of knowledge ranging from the human and legal rights of individual clients to detailed knowledge of organizations, decision-making procedures, power, and system change. A superintendent of a large residential institution recently stated that his best insurance policy is his advocacy staff.

There are no formal training arrangements to prepare individuals for full-time advocacy roles. The following list includes some of the skills that full-time advocates need:

1. Client-centered Data
   a. identification of needs
   b. data collection procedures
   c. record-keeping
   d. normalization principles
   e. legal rights
   f. human rights
2. Organizational and Human Service Systems
   a. system responsibilities
   b. system resources
   c. locating sources of power
   d. identifying decision-making processes
   e. influencing organizations
   f. standards
   g. program-monitoring
3. Organizing Citizens for Action
4. Use of Public Media

Many of the skill areas listed above could be obtained in institutions of higher education. But there are a number of characteristics of universities that interfere with their ability to provide advocacy training. The first limitation concerns the resistance of most university preservice training programs to interact with the service-delivery system. Institutions of higher learning tend to value and reinforce research and writing, university-based training, and service, in that order. Most training programs have strong residency requirements and students go to the university for training. In many instances while students are being trained, they have limited interaction with the service-delivery system, and in some training programs they have none. Advocacy training ought to take place within the context of personal experience. A comprehensive advocacy training design would require extensive interaction in the delivery system by both trainers and students. Until universities reconsider their priorities and value service along with research and university-based training, it is unlikely that university faculty will invest the amount of time needed in order to be effective enablers in advocacy training.

Another limitation of universities in advocacy training concerns the universities' resistance to changing their curriculum and their usual focus on learning in the classroom in contrast to field-based learning. There is so much variance in human need and human-service systems that very few advocacy principles can be dealt with apart from experience. Given the insulation of universities and the traditional patterns of university-based training, it unlikely that there are many university staff members with the ability and background to provide training. Directors of practicum or outreach may be most appropriate in many instances.

When one looks at a university from an advocacy perspective, it is likely that an advocate would say that the university might be an advocacy target rather than a mechanism for advocacy training. It is indeed true that university students often require advocacy in order to move through the academic program.

It is unfortunate that universities embody so many of the negative characteristics of large institutions, including inflexibility and resistance to change, unresponsiveness to individual client needs, and a tendency in some instances to tailor their programs for the convenience of staff rather than the needs of students. Too much of the time and energy of universities is aimed at the maintenance of their own systems. Insufficient energy is directed toward understanding and responding to public needs.

Although there are many problems associated with attempts to train advocates in university environments, basic advocacy training should be available for all students headed for careers in the human-service system. It is not suggested that this training should take the form of a full-semester three-hour course in an academic department. Also, the training would need to cut across a variety of departments within the university. It is therefore likely that this training could be performed most effectively by an institute that is detached from any single academic unit.

An advocacy training institute could then offer training in a variety of forms to each academic department. This institute could offer supervised field-based experience to students interested in relating advocacy theory and principles to actual experience.

Territorial training interests within and between departments are recognized here. The common interests of departments in the advocacy training institute would not automatically find mutual attraction. Funding, control of students and curriculum, and institute policy would be of interest to each department and program involved.

Here is an excellent opportunity to illustrate the inside-outside, dual, integrative approach in the governance of the institute. An outside constituency base would be important in advising the institute on its policies and priorities for advocacy training.

The particular organizational arrangement of such an institute would, of course, depend upon the individual university situation. It is not the purpose here to detail the features of such an organization but rather to note the potential importance of the university in advocacy training and some of the issues involved in activating that potential.

In overcoming the barriers to advocacy training in the university, however, two specific issues here need emphasis. First, as with any good program planning, those to be involved in implementing the program should be involved in the planning. Here this may include outside consumers and students in addition to personnel and budget components of the university administration as well as representatives of the academic departments of professional schools. Second, an active advisory body with reasonable consumer or constituent representation is essential. This group has its own advocacy function to perform in policy disputes, for example, where the advocacy training mission of the institute is in jeopardy.

The potential for advocacy training in a university, as indicated here, is great. If within-system advocacy programs are to develop, these training resources in the university must be effectively accessed.

SUMMARY AND CONCLUSION

An attempt has been made in this chapter to identify advocacy needs, advocacy activity, advocacy training activity, and advocacy training needs. It is clear that, despite the growing need and interest in advocacy activity, training arrangements are haphazard and fragmented. Part of the problem stems from the fact that advocacy activity as it interacts with the human-service system and with the larger social system is not yet clearly defined. Additionally, because advocacy activity strives to render the human-service system accountable and responsive to its clients, the service system is often threatened by the concept. It is, therefore, difficult for advocacy programs and projects to access from the system the support that is needed for both service and training. When resources are limited they are directed toward service, and training is viewed as an unaffordable luxury.

One must ask the question: to what extent can advocates be trained or to what extent is it a life style? From the writers' viewpoint there is a life style that is well suited to advocacy activity. Among the personal characteristics that make up that style are: independence, the ability to cope with ambiguity, the strength to cope with isolation and criticism within an organization, the confidence to make decisions based on beliefs rather than external peer or system pressure, and the ability to identify closely with a client and view the system through the client's eyes. Given these characteristics it is likely that training could greatly improve the effectiveness of an advocate.

The concept of advocacy needs to be shared with a variety of organizations with connections that range from local to state to federal levels. On one hand consumer organizations should play a key role, identifying themselves as advocacy organizations. The consumer organization perspective has two weaknesses. First, an alliance of consumer organizations is needed that cuts across categorical groupings. Second, the consumer organizations lack an alliance with the delivery system. The advocacy concept needs to be embedded in a variety of organizations that have the potential of bringing together consumers and service providers. Institutions of higher education could function as a catalyst between consumers and providers. It remains to be seen whether universities will respond to the need for closer ties with the delivery system.

Another trend that can help to bring about an alliance between the public and private sectors are the mandates of state and federal legislation to include consumer representatives on planning boards at the state and federal levels. Councils for the developmentally disabled are examples of such an organization. Such a council exists in each state across the nation. Their mandate is to develop comprehensive statewide plans for handicapped persons within their state. The council consists of representatives from the consumer sector, service providers and state agencies. Many of the councils have adopted an advocacy perspective, and some literature has been developed on these councils as advocacy mechanisms (Paul, Neufeld, Wiegerink 1975). What the councils need is sufficient money to implement advocacy programs supported by systematic training arrangements designed to develop advocacy into an extensive social movement.

In conclusion, advocacy training should be developed as a vehicle not only to develop specific advocacy skills, but also to develop a social movement with public and private alliances. Training arrangements should be closely related to the service-delivery system and rely heavily on experiences that point directly to individual clients. Unlike traditional university training programs, advocacy training should de-emphasize preservice and emphasize in-service training. Whether influencing changes in organizational structures and/or policies or representing the specific interests of the individual, the ultimate success or failure of advocacy depends on its ability to effect changes that meet the needs of individuals. Action ceases to be advocacy when an individual's need is compromised for the program or the system. Thus, the central interest of advocacy training must be client centered, whether that interest is approached from inside or outside the system or both and whether through organizational change or directly.

Table 8.1 summarizes the information presented in the chapter. It

Table 8.1

ADVOCACY TRAINING CHART

Training Need	Training Organization	Advocate Rules	Training Period	Training Content
Citizen or Volunteer Advocates	Voluntary Organizations	Case Advocates Board Members	In-service	Client communication Normalization Human, legal rights Monitoring procedures Data collection System resources Negotiation procedures
Service Provider/ Advocate A dual role	Service Delivery System	Case Advocates	In-service	Client communication Normalization Human, legal rights Monitoring procedures Data collection System resources Negotiation procedures Parent communication Community communication
	University		Preservice	
Full-time Advocates	University	Ombudsman	Preservice	Client-centered Data: identification of needs, data collection procedures, record keeping, normalization principles, legal rights, human rights. Organizational and Human Services Systems: system responsibilities and resources, locating sources of power, identifying decision-making processes, influencing organizations, standards, monitoring. Organizing Citizens for Action. Use of Public Media.

is organized according to the training need, training organization, role of the advocate for which training is provided, whether the training period is preservice or in-service, and the training content. Three types of advocacy are included: (1) citizen or volunteer advocacy, (2) service provider/advocacy, and (3) full-time advocacy.

REFERENCE

Paul, James L.; Wiegerink, Ronald; and Neufeld, G. Ronald, eds. *Advocacy: A Role for DD Councils.* DD/TAS, FPG Child Development Center, University of North Carolina, Chapel Hill, 1975.

9

Advocacy Program Development

JAMES L. PAUL

ISSUES THAT HAVE BEEN FOUND TO BE CRITICAL in the development of advocacy programs include the quality of planning and the careful installation of an advocacy program into the socio-political environment in which it is to function. Planning an advocacy program does not stop with the initiation of a design, which in turn is not finished when construction begins. One of the several reasons why this is true is that an advocacy program has no fixed or static set of rules to govern its development. Another factor relates to the dynamic quality of environments in which advocacy occurs. As those environments change, the response to the advocacy program will change. Those changes keep the advocate close to the drawing board.

There are basically three questions that need to be answered at the outset of the development of an advocacy program: (1) What are the needs you wish to address? (2) What is your political base of support? (3) What are your priorities?

ASSESSING NEED

One of the best ways to define advocacy is in terms of the needs you are seeking to meet. It is in the statement of needs that the language employed tends to develop. It is in the statement of needs that the basis of linkage and liaison with the human-service systems is found. It is in the statement of needs that you get the attention of the private sector.

The needs assessment does not have to be a highly technical or esoteric activity. It can be, and indeed should be, a way of establishing contact with the community. It is a process for involving the community and for setting the tone of the advocacy program. It is by definition a system for educating the advocate. Clear need statements become boundaries for advocacy activities that facilitate rather than inhibit advocacy activity. When trying to answer the question how, it is important for the advocate to be able to answer the question why.

ASSESSING POLITICAL SUPPORT

Politicians are advocates. They are not necessarily advocates for children or even for human interests. They are, however, a part of a power arrangement that is organized to accomplish certain ends. They speak for a constituency.

Part of the problem in human services is that too much independent authority has been delegated to bureaucrats. Bureaucracies become separated from the people they are established to serve. If the advocacy program is totally encompassed by an existing bureaucratic umbrella, then the advocacy program must live with the rules, constraints, and limitations of that bureaucracy. To the extent that advocacy is concerned with a better fit between human services and those served by those systems, and to the extent that advocacy is an effort to promote accountability more toward the person served than toward the bureaucracy, the exclusive bureaucratic umbrella is usually inadequate.

Political support for an advocacy program, a power base, is absolutely essential. If the advocacy program is to have any character to distinguish it from other conventional bureaucracies, that character must be fashioned out of work between the open political community and the usually less open professional service systems.

Certainly the political functions of advocacy can be overstated and can in reality be overexercised. There is no more gained by advocacy's becoming just another political system than in its becoming just another bureaucracy. A delicate balance has to be struck between patience in facilitating the human goals of the bureaucracy and the careful use of power in initiating change.

Political systems should have an opportunity to advocate for the rights of people. The advocate can provide politicians and the citizenry with information not ordinarily available to them, thus introducing alternative courses of action they might not otherwise consider.

The advocate can also be exploited by either the bureaucracy or the political system when either has interests that are outside the legitimate scope of advocacy. Bureaucrats can, for example, exploit the advocate's credibility in solving problems in the system, especially if the advocate is paid by the system. This is not a simple issue.

A power base outside the bureaucracy is essential. Just as essential is the sparing and discretionary use of that power base. The assumption that existing support and good will in the bureaucracy is sufficient and that an outside power base is not necessary is probably naive. An advocacy program needs a constituency and must provide an opportunity for people to learn about human services and needs. This can and should facilitate the work of the human-service system. It can be a central focus for the advocacy system.

Much of the power base for the advocacy program must be developed as it goes along and on the basis of the advocacy program's own merit. But the power base must exist in some form before any serious advocacy activity is initiated.

ESTABLISHING PRIORITIES

In order to begin the advocacy program, the advocate must have some sense of a plan, some rather specific feeling for the needs to be met over a long time period and a more specific understanding of what has to be accomplished immediately. Long-range goals are met only if the shoulders of short-range accomplishments are strong enough for them to stand on.

Establishing priorities is something the advocate will have to do more than once. It is part of the advocate's interaction with the community, since he or she cannot decide independently what is most important. The community must be involved in those decisions not just for the sake of involvement itself, but because the advocate does not have enough information to make all those decisions alone. Decisions that affect the lives and resources of people must be made, as much as possible, by those people. The advocate must have a picture of the advocacy program sufficiently in mind so that a logical sequence of events can be developed. The first priority may well be to develop an ad hoc arrangement for getting some of the community together to help the advocate make decisions about priorities.

CRUCIAL DECISIONS

In the preceding section on what one needs to know in beginning an advocacy program, several decisions were implied. This section will describe crucial decisions that must be made with careful attention. These decisions are not necessarily unique to advocacy, but they have been found to be basic to the quality of the advocacy program that emerges.

Who Is Accountable?

The question here might be rephrased: Who can put you out of business? Your support group and your direction of accountability are not always in the same direction. It is of course desirable that they flow in the same direction. In an advocacy program you are more likely than in almost any other program to experience this kind of division of interest.

Accountability decisions are built into the organizational structure of your advocacy program. That accountability and that structure is constantly influenced by your behavior as an advocate. The character and style of the advocacy program as well as the freedom and prerogative of the advocate are facilitated or constrained by the accountability network of the program.

The decisions, then, that are made at the outset, and are reviewed about the accountability of the advocate and the advocacy programs, are crucial decisions. It is hard for the advocate to perform his work when he is worried about being fired.

Who Needs to be Involved?

Several things govern decisions about who needs to be involved in maintaining the advocacy program. The timing of involvement is as important as selecting the right people to be involved.

The most willing and the most available are not necessarily the most appropriate to be involved. The enthusiasm of the most available people can in fact be very deceptive and lead you into inappropriate deductions about the quality of support you may anticipate in the community.

One thing that should guide your decision about who should be involved is some model or philosophy of what advocacy is and how it should work in the community. That is, decisions about involving community members should be based on some rationale related to the advocacy mission, and procedurally how you get the community involved in advocacy.

The decision about who should be involved also should relate to the known political idiosyncracies of the community. It would be as much a mistake to ignore or otherwise fail to involve politically significant members of the community who wish to be involved as it would be to let the effort become coopted by a single interest. In this fine distinction, nothing will serve the advocate better than careful diplomacy.

The decision about who is to be involved, and in what role, can sometimes not be made in terms of a specific philosophy, purpose of the project, or even political features of the community. Sometimes it just seems the right thing to do. While the advocate should not develop and run the program solely on the basis of his feelings and hunches, his intuitions do have a legitimate place in his work. There are times when that is all he does have, or so it feels to him.

It is not good policy to get into the habit of justifying decisions solely on the basis of "it felt right," but it is good human policy to pay attention to one's feelings and give them a place in the decision-making process.

How Will You Know if You Are on Track?

The central point here is not the decision that you are on track or not on track but rather the prior decision about how you will know, by what criteria you will judge, or by what process you will determine whether or not you are on track, and if not, how far off you are. This is not just a formal evaluation question. It is true that the care with which the needs are stated at the outset will certainly help in answering the question of whether you are doing what you set out to do. That information will also help in assessing whether what you set out to do still fits. Your experience may tell you that what you should be doing is different from what you set out to do. The issue here is how you will deal with those kinds of decisions.

Part of the answer to the question of whether you are on track or not is answerable in objective terms. Perhaps not so obvious is the fact that part of the answer to that question is subjective: "I feel we are right." This kind of latitude needs to be built in from the beginning.

But where do you quit on a hunch? Where do you draw the line between persistence and perseveration? For the advocate, much of the guidance for deciding whether he is on or off track must come from a core community, the advocate's community, that may be only one other person. Depending on the project, it will have to involve other advocates, and, depending on the issue, it may have to involve the larger community. Mechanisms such as councils for children or community advocacy councils can provide some of this kind of guidance and feedback.

What Is Your Real Power Base?

The power base for the program will vary over time. It will vary in strength and in some instances even in location. The important issue here, however, is whom you can count on when the chips are down.

It is not typically in the interest of the advocate or his mission to allow the chips to be down. When they are, negotiation has ceased. When battle lines are drawn, change is brought about more on the basis of a dynamic of force and concession than on the basis of learning, persuasion, and agreement. Sometimes, however, the chips are down and they have to be to save the integrity of the advocacy mission. That is, a right of the child is at stake and no other alternatives are available.

It has been earlier pointed out that the discreet use of power is important with the emphasis being on discretion even at the point where power assistance is needed. Serious damage can be done by flaunting it. The advocate must keep his own ego needs in check. Flexing one's muscles will not bring admiration from many for long. The advocate must, at best, broker the power and help it focus on the problem; in this manner the confrontation and the resolution occurs within the community's own system of power and balance. It salvages for both sides, when issues are reduced to sides, redemptive possibilities of growing and learning.

If this occurs the advocate must accept his own knowledge that he has succeeded and not go beyond that and claim public victory. This should be not more than a step in the process of advocacy in the community which facilitates future advocacy. Your power base will be

strengthened if you treat it gently. If you have not been an acknowledged victor, you will not have to waste a lot of future time dealing with
the fallout of the victim's ego loss.

It is important to recognize that your real power base is not necessarily your public power base. The point here has to do with style, not
with secrecy. The advocate's credibility is always his strongest tool.

Minimum Standards for Continuing

Since the rhythm of advocacy activity is erratic and the drain on
morale substantial, it is important to decide as much as possible under
what condition you would give up the project. While it is not good to
dwell on this kind of point—that is, what kinds of things could be so
bad as to cause me to quit—it is good to know where the floor is so you
can know how far up you are when you are feeling down.

There are many personal matters that could cause an individual
advocate to pursue a different course. These would include, for example,
his own lack of energy or the jeopardy his advocacy might place on his
continuing family structure. There are also less personal, issue-based
criteria by which one could decide when advocacy programs should no
longer continue.

When advocacy work is hollow, without resolve or meaning to
those involved, it is probably dead. To define what being dead is could
facilitate a later decision that the thing is dead, and it is therefore time
to move on to other things; knowing that it is not dead will allow you
to take the necessary remedial action to stop its apparent dying.

This is the framework in which the advocate must consider those
decisions which involve risking the entire project. The advocate must
pick very carefully the cross he or the project is willing to die on.

Critical Information Network

One of the significant decisions that must be made early and reviewed periodically has to do with the basic information network of the
advocacy project. One of the ways the advocate has of developing and
maintaining his credibility is through keeping people informed. He cannot possibly keep in his head all the time all the information related to
advocacy needs and advocacy activities. He must therefore have some

kind of record system which facilitates his acquisition of information and transmitting it. A record system that coopts the advocate's time for advocacy activity and wraps him up in paper is not facilitative. Keeping good records, however, must be viewed as one aspect of the advocacy activity. A good record system can be a very substantial part of the advocate's accountability.

What kinds of records? That, in large part, relates to the question of for whom and for what purposes the records are kept, which raises the issue of determining the critical information network. Who needs to know? When do they need to know? How do they need to be informed?

This network has both formal and informal dimensions and both public and private dimensions. There are some things that everyone needs not to know. There are also some things that everyone needs not to know. Some of the same information that could be used by certain people to accomplish advocacy ends could be used by other people to exploit the person for whom advocacy is being attempted. The advocate must attend to the exploitative potential of information as much as the facilitative potential of information. There are laws that govern some aspects of selecting and disseminating information, specifically with regard to privacy and confidentiality. Other issues are not dealt with as a matter of law but they do pose very specific ethical questions. The advocate is well advised to have some forum in which he can deal over time with the rightness-wrongness dimension of information and information dissemination. Within this general context he is also well advised to have adequate legal counsel.

As a general rule, information about a person belongs most directly to that person. Usage of that information, therefore, should be with the awareness and consent of that person or that person's duly authorized representative. In some instances the advocate is the person's representative relative to the usage of information by other people.

The critical information network can be thought of as the cognitive system of advocacy. There should be some general fit between the elements or components of the advocacy system and the information network.

Role of Consumers

It is not sufficient to simply decide that consumers will be involved. The decision has to be extended to include the questions: Who is a consumer? How will they be involved? When will they be involved?

The philosophy and organization of the advocacy program should indicate who will be involved in basic decision-making and policy formulation in the project. How well this is thought through and implemented will be a critical factor and perhaps the most critical factor in the success or failure of the advocacy program.

One approach is to institutionalize consumer or, more broadly, citizen involvement. Organizational mechanisms reflect this kind of institutionalization of the role. Some work well if the institutional form fits the goals and objectives of the advocacy program and if those goals also fit the perceptions of the citizens involved. If there is a perceptual misfit, there will be major problems. The participating members must share the vision of what the institutional form is intended to accomplish.

Institutionalizing mechanisms to handle constituency roles, for example, can facilitate and protect the credibility of the advocacy mission if it works properly. It can also be an Achilles Heel both to the community support and to the morale of the program.

Less formal ad hoc arrangements are in some instances more desirable, but there are risks here also. Suffice it to say that the role of the consumer and of the citizenry at large must be carefully considered, and the decision to handle that role with any formal organization must also be carefully thought through.

Policy and the Public Media

Decisions have to be made about the public media which can be an instrument in education and a tool for involving the citizenry. It can be a power resource, but it is subject to exploitation. If exploited, beware of the backlash.

Many issues related to public information have been described in the preceding material. It is separated here as a policy issue about which some action or decision needs to be taken early because it is so important.

It is probably a mistake to adopt any extreme position on the public media, that is, to strive to stay always out of the public media or to strive to stay always in the public media. In most instances people need to know about the advocacy programs, but they do not need to be fatigued by them.

There are obvious political and legal considerations in developing policy on involving the public media. There are also perhaps not-so-obvious psychological considerations which contribute to or detract from a successful advocacy strategy.

A newspaper editor can be a very important cornerstone to the advocacy program's usually silent power base. To be an advocate for the advocate he must be informed but must also share in the general strategy of interfacing the advocacy program with the total citizenry. Timing, for example, is crucial, but it must be judged more in terms of the internal interest of the advocacy program than the newspaper's getting first coverage of the story.

The critical information network described above is usually small enough so that more detail and more dialog is possible. There is also more tolerance for error and more opportunity to correct mistakes. There is more control and more opportunity to insure that the message you intended and thought you sent was the message that was received. This kind of control, tolerance for error, and opportunity to adjust messages does not exist as much in the public media.

Boundaries between Advocacy and Service

One of the most pervasive conceptual problems for advocacy has been the distinction between advocacy and service. We think more in service terms of providing something than we do in accountability terms of assuring the availability and credibility of what is provided. Many have sought to make of advocacy another special service. Words for the accountability functions, which is most of what advocacy is about, have not come easily.

One of the decisions that must be made early is how the advocacy program will function in relation to the service programs and how its functioning will be described. It must be described in a way that it can be understood by those whose support for the advocacy program is sought. It must also be described in ways that sufficiently delineate its boundaries from service systems such that productive interchange with the bureaucracy is possible. Finally, it must be described in terms that are clear enough that all know what the advocacy program and the advocate will be held accountable for.

One could think about two major systems of influence that have impact on the lives of children. One is the parenting system and the other is the institutional care-taking and service systems. Both include functions such as caring for, protecting, educating, controlling, and correcting. There is a division of labor and a division of responsibility and authority, either legally specified or socially understood, between these two major forces. The advocacy functions are usually grafted onto the boundary area between them, and sometimes the advocate gets wedged between the two. Advocacy then must be differentiated from both the institutional service system and the family-parenting system.

10

Advocacy and the Advocate

JAMES L. PAUL

CHILD ADVOCACY takes much of its meaning from the personal encounter. That is, there is inequity or abuse in the encounter between a child or group of children and one or more adults or adult-administered systems. That inequity or abuse has been viewed as the consequence of the arrangement between people in a system rather than deliberate, goal-oriented activity. This has been called a "bad fit."

Since it is the child-other encounter that contributes directly to the problems for both the child and others, it is that personal encounter that must be changed. Intervention into a situation to improve or correct the child-other fit is called "advocacy."

Another significant encounter from which advocacy takes its meaning is that between the child and tasks the child is expected to perform. Such a child-task encounter includes the environment as well as the goals, activities, and materials or equipment comprising the task. In its broadest sense, this is the child-curriculum encounter.

Both the child-other and the child-task encounter typically involve changing the system or the arrangement in which the child is involved. Both encounters are personal, since (1) they involve the personal, the developing child, and (2) they involve changing something that others are involved in and in which they typically have personal vested interests.

Both the object of the change, that is the *arrangement,* and the purpose of the change, the major source of specific objectives which guide the change, that is the *child,* make personal demands on any change agent. It is this demand that is at the center of any consideration of

141

understanding advocates. Any beginning development of a psychology of advocates must incorporate an understanding of the nature of the advocacy tasks and the demands these tasks place upon the person of the advocate. The following discussion focuses attention on this topic. It should not be considered an exhaustive discussion but only a beginning to suggest some of the dimensions of complexity involved. The discussion is organized around two basic themes: the advocate as individual, and the advocate and others. Others include children, the advocate's family, professionals and bureaucrats, and the community.

The Advocate as Individual

One of the most basic and pervading themes with which the advocate must deal is that of *boundaries* of professional role as well as personal identity. What is the line that divides what I can do from what I cannot? What is it that I am responsible for in contrast to areas in which I have no accountability? Where will I draw the line in professional rationalization for practices that have serious moral implications? Where will I place the fulcrum that balances the child's interest and the system's interest? How far will I go in pursuing a strong conviction which has verification only in my own head? How far does the parents' prerogative extend? How close will I allow myself to get to the child? How much am I willing to risk?

The boundaries of who I am and what I do as an advocate are not set in place by a theory or a professional code. They are also not set in place permanently. They are not necessarily put in place publicly, although there is certainly a need to move in this direction.

At this point both the advocate and the advocacy process are vulnerable. If there are moral constants, they do not always fit. If there are situational constants, their meanings vary. The more freedom I have to decide, the more chance to be wrong, the more lonely I become. Freedoms in this dimension quickly become constraints or are experienced as such. The more I can, or must, decide the more I must defend— morally, legally, and alas, bureaucratically. The absence of givens, rules, or boundaries is the Achilles Heel of the advocate and the potential lance of the system the advocate seeks to change.

Certainly the advocate is not in a moral or technical vacuum and is not constantly without guidance. The advocate, however, more than those in common helping professions, is placed in a position of deciding the source of his or her guidance. More than others, the advocate is required to determine with less guidance, his or her identity and course of action. Perhaps more than most, the advocate is required to change that determination.

It is suggested here that (1) the advocate's primary source of information is the child and the child's situation; (2) the advocate is required to rely heavily on his or her own resources in order to understand how best to relate to that situation; and (3) the absence of common boundaries of work, which theoretically increase the freedom to define and intervene in a situation, increases the advocate's ultimate accountability and, therefore, the care with which action must be taken.

Another significant aspect of the advocate's dilemma in defining self and placing work in proper perspective to the human-service network and the child's ecology has to do with *authority*. While this is another manifestation of the boundary issue, it is discussed separately here because of its importance.

Who speaks for the child when the child cannot speak for himself? Who decides when the child can speak for himself? Do parents "own" the child? Does the teacher have exclusive authority in "educational matters"?

Professionals have staked out claims to rather specific parts of a child, including the mental health part, welfare part, health part, educational part. Settings have laid claim to parts of the child's life on a *de facto* basis of the child's occupancy. Institutions do this.

Still, the major claimants for the whole child are parents. Their prerogatives, generally, supersede the prerogatives of others.

Most of those who work with or otherwise make decisions about children have a legal basis for their authority. Where no clear legal basis exists, there is commonly a clear professional basis with public sanction. There is much authority over the lives of children spread across the policies, bylaws, rules, guidelines, and procedures of bureaucracies.

One has only to get involved in advocacy for a child to discover there is a relatively specific understanding of who has authority, when, and where. While many bureaucracies envelop the lives of children, an advocate will quickly discover that the child has no authority at all.

Where then does the advocate's work begin or end? What is the advocate's authority? What is the source of that authority if there is any?

The most accurate answer is that the advocate has no authority. The advocate does, however, have power—in the argument developed, the evidence collected to support it, and the people who hear it. The power of the advocate can reside in the authority of the school board if that is the relevant body that can take action if given sufficient appropriate information. The advocate's power can be the chief administrator of an agency, the power of the governor's office, or the power of the courts.

Primarily, however, the advocate's power must reside in the people whose confidence and respect come from the work done by and the positions taken by the advocate. It is the ability to communicate, to get the right people together, to *effectively* assist citizens that is the basis of the advocate's credibility, which is, ultimately, the source of the advocate's authority.

The executive and judicial branches of government are *resources* to be used when immediate solutions at the neighborhood level fail or when their pursuit at a local level does not make sense conceptually, such as the right to education which has been pursued in the courts as a class action. Most advocacy must take place around the child, with the people directly involved, dealing with specific issues. That is where the action is, and that is where the authority must be.

This base of authority sounds better than it feels. It is not a comfortable bureaucratic niche! It is tenuous and vulnerable to, albeit well-intended, sabotage by such reputable members of child-serving systems as the mental health center director or the school principal.

This situation contributes to the relative stability experienced by the advocate, who must determine the boundaries of advocacy work in a process of developing a constituency from which support and authority for such work will be derived. The mental health of the advocate as well as his or her effectiveness is fundamentally related to the integrity of that process, which never ends. The reverse holds equally true.

THE ADVOCATE AND OTHERS

The Advocate's Family

The advocate, concerned with the child-others and child-tasks adaptations, has his or her own life adaptations. The advocate-others and advocate-tasks adaptations are also changing and subject to noise or bad fit. As with the child, or anyone else for that matter, difficulty in one area usually affects another. Similarly, very good fit in one helps nourish the other. That is, if work goes very well, relationships tend to benefit from that success. If relationships are very supportive, there is usually more energy available for work tasks.

Most of the advocate's work is in personal relationships. The advocate-others adaptation, therefore, includes most of the advocate's own work and personal life. The boundary here is one of the most difficult of all to establish. It is probably only an arbitrary determination at best and is constantly changing. Boundaries in the advocate's head are not always in the heads of the advocate's family. Those boundaries are even less in the heads of the children, others in their life, and the timing of events that require assistance.

Since there is no clear public bureaucracy of advocacy with roles which neighbors understand, it is not always possible for the advocate to communicate what is done—even to his or her own family. Usually, in response to the family's question, "what do you do?" the advocate gives examples and talks about why and what he or she does. The family feeling together with or connected to the work relaxes until a neighbor, a teacher, or someone else asks "what does your husband (wife) do?" Lost for specifics and for classification, the question is recycled: "Tell me again, what do you do?"

This contributes to the advocate's identity problem. He must be assured while he reassures his family that he is legitimately employed and involved in respectable work. This even when he is losing ground "out there."

There are many variations on this situation, of course. Sometimes the family gets involved enough to develop their own advocate identity. This has good and bad implications.

The personal demand in advocacy is sufficiently great that the advocate must have a source of support for himself and a human space for retreat where the problems of others do not occupy central attention. Advocates need advocacy and must, at times, advocate for themselves.

It is very difficult to be on call for 24 hours a day and find that there is no time to get away. This is certain death. If the advocate is exploited—and he or she will be—and does not make time for himself, he will lose energy, perspective, and effectiveness. This is one entry into a cycle of withdrawal, depression, resentment, hostility, and failure.

Another aspect of the advocacy work involves the *"person*-ality" of the advocacy process. That is, the advocate cannot hide behind many agency rules and procedures. The advocate's desk is not always located between himself and the people he works with. In some ways advocacy is caring that has not yet been institutionalized. Institutions, for whatever their ills, provide a certain protection for people. Here advocacy has its hazards. While the advocate establishes personal boundaries, it is naive to assume that what he intends in his behavior and the perceived intentions of that behavior will always be the same. Rumors are like wildfire and more damaging.

What implications does this have for the family? In addition to the constructive definition of the work, there must be the defensive protection of the integrity of the image. This situation obviously varies with the family's life style, the issue involved, the culture of the community, and the history the advocate has with the community.

Another implication of the person-ality of the role involves the family's feelings about sharing the affections and personal attention of the advocate. This difficulty can arise in several ways. One of the most constant is "You are supposed to be an advocate for children, what about your own?" What follows, then, is an account of a problem one of the children is having, which surfaced the "whose territory are you" feelings.

The family must be a primary source of support for the advocate. To keep that together, it is essential that the advocate develop ways that fit his style and that of his family to update where they are, what they are doing, how they are doing together, and to create ways of improving their relationships. This is easier said than done. While there are known helpful ways of doing this, some work is needed to document ways in which process can occur as it relates to the uniqueness of the advocate's role. This is a major cornerstone of the advocacy process.

THE ADVOCATE WITH PROFESSIONALS
AND BUREAUCRATS

The advocate will quickly find himself placed in a defensive posture if care is not taken. Never underestimate the importance of place to people. The territory, including professional work space and responsibility, of a person is a major portion of a person's social body. One does not invade it, challenge its functions, or, even by implication, question its integrity without reaction. Just because reaction is not immediate or overt, do not assume it is not present. The body is presumed to be complete, a characteristic that plays havoc with interagencism.

These observations are not intended to be cynical or flippant. The territorial "instincts" of bureaucracies and those who populate bureaucratic organizations, for example, have been described extensively in other literature. The need to own, to have a secure niche, and to be safe from unpredictable intrusion is a common human need. It has many manifestations in the need of organizations to survive, and it is not being disclaimed or criticized here. Rather, it is noted as a characteristic of the organizational and professional environment in which the advocate must develop his or her work.

One manifestation of this problem is in the generic attack on advocacy. "I'm an advocate; all the people who work in this agency are advocates—what makes you different?" The implication is that the name of the work, advocacy, is arrogant. It is probably not true that all who work in that agency are advocates (but you do not say that). It is true that the language of advocacy leaves much to be desired in engendering the togetherness the philosophy espouses (that you can say). A better vocabulary is needed if words are getting in our way. Successful attack on the words has, in some quarters, been considered successful attack on what advocacy is about. If this writing serves no other purpose, it will help erase the ignorance of that assumption.

Another understandable challenge the advocate is likely to face is that of credentials. "What is your degree in?" This is an attempt to get a handle on where to place you on the professional landscape and to understand what kind of behavior might be expected. It is an attempt to identify you in relation to me. Depending on the timing, place, and information already available to the person asking the question, it can be a rhetorical question, a putdown.

A related question involves your experience. You will not get questions about the quality of your experience. The questions are how much experience, in what settings, doing what.

All the questions from the organizations and professionals involve the basic issue of boundary. They can tell you their boundaries. They want to know yours. Attempting to work as advocates within the system has as one of its major challenges that of defining boundaries that are workable.

The Advocate and the Community

When boundaries are not manifest in the system, the community will pursue the vocabulary, the definition, or the history of the role and, if necessary, generate a connection it can understand. The community's first concerns are with *what* are you doing and *why*. The motivation is important. It is at this level of the advocate-community encounter that trust and credibility are developed. This is the roadbed for what has been referred to as community entry. The question of what you are *really* up to runs far in front of how well you can do it.

The importance of this situation for understanding the advocate role lies in the personal corollary of the community's question. The question of what are you up to is one part of a two-part question. The other part is: Who are you? What are your values? What can you be trusted to do? To not do? What are your boundaries?

Familiar bureaucracy helps the community answer questions about personal types. The advocate must continually speak for himself. His actions continually speak of himself.

In his struggle with boundaries, one of the most difficult is that between advocacy and adversarial activity. When does it no longer make sense to negotiate and persuade? When is it time for confrontation? For a lawyer?

Obviously many considerations are important here. The issue in this discussion, however, is the role the community can play in setting up the situation in which a decision is necessary. What may appear to be an advocacy issue involving a child can be an issue centered more directly upon the advocate. Resistance to remedying a situation can become a contest of wills between the advocate and members of the community. This can occur because the conflict has developed between the advocate and community's members or interests. It can also occur because of uncertainty in the community as to who the advocate is, that is, his or her boundaries.

Community members will test their boundaries to discover the advocate's boundaries if they are unclear. Such testing may range from a desire to know and get things straight to attempts to impeach the advocate or otherwise move him or her out of the community.

The community frequently participates with bureaucrats and professionals in attempts to remove ambiguity or threat posed by the advocate. One way this occurs, for example, is in the moves of human-service agencies to control or otherwise coopt the advocate. This may take the form of budgeting arrangements or of administrative or "professional" accountability. If the advocate has not thought through his or her accountability boundary, others will decide.

It is in this broad but very basic area that the advocate and the advocacy process can be sidetracked and ultimately derailed. The advocate-centered advocacy issue can be volatile and/or malignant. It can so coopt the time and energy of the advocate that child-centered advocacy becomes a side car left at the station, a history that the advocate refers to in defending the present situation. This is an untenable situation that can be very demoralizing to the advocate, who then loses freedom in pursuing better boundaries and maturing as an advocate because his perspective and energy are so absorbed in defending his own boundary that the community wants to change.

Help is almost always needed where such conflict and standoff occur. The advocate can be exiled within the community and left to run in place. This can be as devastating as destructive conflict. Both erode credibility.

The Advocate with the Child

The advocate's relationship with the child is almost always the easiest and the most consistently rewarding. Given the environment of advocacy, it is easy for the advocate to ask too much from the child in rewarding the work of advocacy. In most instances it is the child's improved situation that must be the source of reward for the advocate—not the advocate's relationship with the child.

The child is the primary source of information about how he is doing. He is not necessarily the exclusive evaluator of the goodness or badness of how he is doing, what he needs, and what he is getting. The child cannot afford to have the advocate lose this perspective.

The advocate's relationship with the child is typically the most dependable and the most consistent. In some situations, it is the most important aspect of the advocacy work. More often it is not.

There are no universal boundaries or rules that govern this distinction. What does the advocate do when what he needs and what the child needs are in conflict? Sometimes this is a problem of timing. Sometimes it is a problem of the advocate's ego. It is an excuse if the advocate can facilitate other more enduring relationships for the child, such as with his father, and needs to not recognize the opportunity to do so. The advocate must adapt to the fact that his work with the child directly may be the least significant thing he can do for the child.

The advocate must be rewarded by his work and his rewards must be related to the children. The point here has specifically to do with the perspective the advocate must maintain.

To review what has been said to this point, the advocate takes as his or her orienting framework the mutual adaptation of children and their environments. Those environments primarily involve people and tasks. It is the work of the advocate to improve the quality of those adaptations.

The advocate is himself an adaptive member of a community with work to do and certain resources available. The quality of his own adaptations contributes to his ability to work as an advocate for children. Who the advocate is—personally—and the nature of the advocacy process interact such that the quality of one cannot be separated from the quality of the other.

The advocate lacks direct authority, and the advocate's power base is the credibility obtained with the community. His principal strategy is negotiation. He has access to the full power of government, but the cost of loading bigger guns to force change is that he moves in to an adversarial mode. That has consequences for the advocate's relationship with the community. That in turn has consequences for how the advocate is able and is allowed to function.

The advocate does not have clear rules or boundaries. His conflict frequently is moral. He has tenuous roots and usually an unstable job base. He must decide who he is, what he will and will not do, what can be compromised, delayed, or tabled, and what is worth the loss of all. Only the advocate can avoid the bureau-ecological traps which can coerce or force him into advocate-centered advocacy rather than child-centered advocacy.

This situation places extra responsibility on the advocate. He must maintain credibility with himself and others in functioning as an effective advocate while surviving in a position that does not always engender support. The following section describes some of the conflicts and problems that affect the advocate's morale.

MORALE OF THE ADVOCATE

Many things affect the advocate's morale: the advocate's own personal needs for support, the depth of his understanding of the problems he is trying to solve, and the nature of his commitment to the work. Morale, however, is an interaction of who the advocate is and the kinds of circumstances that surround him. This section will describe some of those circumstances. The purpose of this section is to suggest some of the areas that can be anticipated by the advocate and by his or her support system in order to reduce the demoralizing impact of these circumstances.

The Problem of Ambiguity

The problem of ambiguity is a problem in clarity of both goals and instrumental activities. The advocate knows intuitively, in spirit, what he is trying to accomplish. That certainty sometimes blurs when he is confronted by a principal, a psychologist, a welfare worker, a policeman, or some other agent of the community service system with a request for specifics. Sometimes that is a request for data or evidence. Sometimes it is a request for rationale: why? Sometimes it is a request for clarification between the advocate's action and a community truism: "Don't you know that parents are responsible and know what is best for their children?" Sometimes it is a cool-out, like: "Yes, I know what you're trying to do but we've been trying to do something about that since Billy started to school here and it is hopeless."

The advocate needs some confirmation of his point of view and the sense of what he is doing. Most offenses against children are not in blatant abuse areas. They are in areas where the rules are not clear, rights not clearly specified, laws not developed, and monitors not functional to make the problems public. This is a double problem for the advocate. First, people do not like to be confronted about these areas. The absence of clear rules makes them anxious and uncomfortable. Second, the advocate will have to settle for something less than a public creed or dogma to guide his or her own thinking.

This ambiguity is difficult to face over time. There is always another point of view with some appeal that ultimately creates doubt in the advocate of himself. This kind of fatigue erodes morale, yet it is essential. A dialog between the advocate and himself and the advocate and others keeps him from habits of institutional thinking and acting. It is nonetheless tiring and demanding of energy that sometimes is not available.

Conflict of Interest

Another aspect of the morale problem has to do with keeping loyalty straight. The advocate's first commitment beyond himself has to be to the person for whom he is advocating. This principle, when applied to real-life advocacy, gets blurred. For example, there are many potential allies for the advocate, and he must have many. Some, however, come at too great an expense. If the advocate must choose between the potential ally and the person for whom he is advocating, his choice has to be relatively clear. What if that ally is an amiable policeman who likes you and wants some help in "getting these kids to mind"? He believes in anything that will work, including making an example out of "the way we deal with hoodlums." You know you will lose his support when you confront him about hassling the "leaders." You know he requires a "practical" answer to delinquency that will work for the "kids of those welfare mothers."

Another conflict of interest or loyalty problem is that involving the agency's perspective on "the client." For example, there is a term, "agency hopper," sometimes used to refer to a person who goes from one agency to another. Agencies sometimes develop the view of the client, whom they have not been able to provide adequate service, as unable to use assistance and ultimately irresponsible. This view of the client as incompetent in using help relieves the agency, in its own view, from feeling responsible for providing services.

The "agency hopper's" perspective is quite different. It is commonly one of not knowing where to go for help, not understanding the relationship between what the agency is providing and the need the person wishes satisfied, being aware of the agency's failure to respond, or needing something from several agencies and having both the wisdom and the will to seek it. Movement from agency to agency, at the "client's" prerogative rather than the agency's, frustrates agencies that wish to do it all or, at a minimum, control the client traffic pattern. "Responsible" clients are those who use us in the ways, at the places, and during the times we specify. To be sure, there are those who manipulate agencies. The important question for the advocate is not if a person manipulates a service system, but why such manipulation is necessary.

If the advocate understands the client's perspective, the advocate may wish to change the time, place, or service provision of the agency. The agency may welcome the advocate's help. He may obtain a better fit between the person's real need and the agency, or he may wear out his welcome as soon as he makes it clear that he is sticking to the person's perspective and not the "bad client" perspective of the agency.

Conciliation can be a celebrated goal of advocacy, but it can also be a sellout. This struggle has consequences for the advocate's morale. There are times when being the good guy is wrong.

The Temptation to Become Cynical

Cynicism can be a defense the advocate adopts when he sees no other place to go and does not yet want to give up. Cynicism is serious because it is a short step from futility. It is a sure sign of a need for help.

Cynicism is usually that condition in which the advocate identifies with the aggressor, the professional, bureaucrat, or the bureaucratic system, and tries to play oneupsman. "We are in this crazy circular argument. You folks [bureaucrats] know you're really not doing anything except ripping off the taxpayer. But then can anybody really help somebody else unless he really wants help? And if he does want help, he'd get it without us. Can professionalized and institutionalized care-giving really work? The bureaucracy provides jobs. Everyone is doing the best he can, given the system and that won't change. Who am I? Am I trying to play God? To be judge and jury? Who can say what is right?"

Cynicism is a very familiar aspect of the psychological field of bureaucracy. It is a common adaptation to impotence, to the uncomfortable distance between expectations and performance.

If it is imbedded deeply enough, cynicism is serious because it does not provide a way out of its own trap. The basic attitude of "show me" does not have a corresponding openness to be shown. It is the openness to information that distinguishes cynicism from doubt and skepticism. The former is part of a psychology of disillusionment and despair. The latter, skepticism, is an attitude that facilitates learning, and it is a basic premise of science. Advocacy has to begin and continue with a constructive skepticism and an openness to learn. Cynicism is counterproductive and ultimately destructive.

The advocate will encounter cynicism in bureaucracy. Cynicism is contagious. Cynicism is debilitating and will keep the advocate's morale low. The cynic's knife can be sharp, his comments caustic. There are times when the advocate is so vulnerable that it is appealing to try to escape his pain. One way to do so is to join "them."

THICK SKIN AND SENSITIVITY

One of the major problems in the work of an advocate is the institutionalized perspective on human needs the advocate finds in the human-service bureaucracy. Systems that habitually provide services provide them on the basis of views of human need, which they seldom re-examine. The assumptions they make about people and about people-needs are frequently not reviewed over time, to say nothing of the failure to review those assumptions client by client.

Part of what the advocate brings to the human-service system is a constructive query of those assumptions. The advocate's questions are rephrased for each person for whom he advocates. The advocate, of course, is vulnerable to advocacy assumptions that are not reviewed and therefore become institutionalized. The advocate is seeking a consideration of each person on the basis of his or her own unique and individual needs and resources. Most human-service systems would claim a similar goal.

Underlying this intellectual sensitivity is the human sensitivity and the ability to respond to the person's needs. Institutions do the same things so often that the connection between those things (programs, procedures, curricula) and the person is not necessarily questioned. Adaptation in some instances must be made by the person receiving the services. It is the recipient with the need in these instances who must be responsive and adaptable, not the service. This remains true despite our realization that increases in certain human needs, which bring a person to seek help, reduce that person's ability to adapt or respond.

The advocate must be able to maintain his or her own responsiveness and sensitivity to individual needs and help promote that sensitivity in the human-service bureaucracy. The paradox, or in many instances the problem, comes in maintaining that sensitivity and openness. There are reasons why bureaucracies are short on sensitivity and adaptability. Some of that reason has to do with the development of defenses for surviving as large and complex organizations. As the advocate continues to work in those systems his or her need for such defense frequently increases.

STYLE IS IMPORTANT

There has been a recurring theme in the material to this point and that has to do with style. The difference between a good advocacy program and a bad one, or a successful advocacy program and an unsuccessful one, may well be not so much in what is done or even why it is done but how the advocate went about doing it. Style is the point at which the advocacy activity joins the type of person doing that activity. The community will see more in the advocate than the advocate ever intends, and it will fail to see many things the advocate wishes very much it would understand. There is no substitute for the advocate's sense of himself and how he is doing with others in the community. If the advocate feels indignant, and sometimes he or she will, it will show. If the advocate feels arrogant, and there is no place for that, others will get the message. If the advocate feels hesitant and uncertain, with any doubt at all— sometimes he or she will and should—others will know. If the advocate cares, and this is essential if the advocate is to work as an advocate very long, there is no way to hide that. The way he dresses, the way he talks, the way he thinks, the hours he works, his attitude toward the government, the way he relates to his family, the way he feels about himself— all are a part of who the advocate is. These attributes connect the goal of the advocacy program with the people in the community. The burden of proof will usually be found on the advocate's own back, not on the community. The following discussion focuses on style variables and the ways in which the advocate and advocacy might be more productively interfaced.

Tactics of Influence

As a general rule the person must make it clear in his behavior that he is more interested in being an advocate than an adversary. The advocate and the adversary play by different rules and usually have very different styles.

The advocate usually needs to get close to interactions so he can understand them sufficiently well that he can provide counsel on how to improve them and reduce transactional discord. This closeness means also being close to teachers, who are viewed by some as being bad, or close to parents, who are viewed by some as being abusive. In order to do that, the advocate must avoid images of being either savior or soldier.

In getting close to troubled transactions, the advocate is on delicate turf. He learns things ordinarily saved for family or very close friends or, in some instances, very carefully developed professional confidences. You do not get close to the enemy to kill him. If you have decided he is the enemy, let him know it before he gives you information on the assumption you are a friend. The advocate of all people must have a very strong, clear, and definite basis for making any judgments about a person apart from that person.

There can be no excuse for exploiting a confidence or abusing a trust. Confidence and trust are basic in the development of successful advocacy.

These kinds of rules are usually applied in relatively well-defined and protected settings. There are lawyer-client, doctor-patient, and clergy-parishioner kinds of protected and privileged communications. The advocate is commonly more out in the open and has fewer institutional sanctions for communication and the protection of information.

There are two sides to this issue. One is the basic protection of human right and the privilege of confidence. The other side of the issue is the political meaning of confidence. Here privacy equals secret equals power equals the basis for suspicion. There is no easy or clearcut method to handle this kind of issue. It can be delicate and obviously can have personal implications. As a general rule the community decodes this kind of behavior in terms of what it knows or understands about the advocate, the way it perceives him. The community's perception of the advocate is in large part a function of the advocate's style.

The advocate has the task of finding a work style that feels comfortable with his own value system and permits the process of advocacy to occur. "Permitting advocacy to occur" means that the advocate behaves in ways that are both acceptable to the community and effective. That is, the advocate must be concerned about the fit of his work with the community value system as well as the efficiency and effectiveness of his or her work in reaching some specified objective. In general, the tactics, strategies, procedures, and philosophies of education, consultation, and persuasion are acceptable. Manipulation, threats, and confrontation are less acceptable. As indicated earlier, power must be used very sparingly even when it is readily available. Threats should be rare and then only gently applied.

The tactics of influence are of primary importance in advocacy. They facilitate the process of advocacy and ultimately give it its public meaning. As a general rule the tactics of advocacy need to be positive, playing to the strength of a person or system and enabling those traits to be further actualized.

Identification with the Bureaucracy

Much of the style of the advocate influences and is influenced by his proximity to the bureaucracy. For purposes of this immediate discussion the bureaucracy is neither good nor bad but rather a fact of organizational life. The relevant question here is how do the advocate and the advocacy enterprise relate to the formal public bureaucracy. The relation, or more accurately the perceived relationship, has a profound impact on the way advocacy is regarded in the community, and that regard will vary with different sectors of the community. The biggest trap of the advocate is excess of identification in either direction—with or against the bureaucracy.

Over-identification with the formal bureaucratic system reduces the likelihood that the advocate can function effectively in informal ways with certain sectors of the community. He may be viewed as an extension of "the system" or "the establishment." The advocate's questions will be viewed as "their questions" and his concerns as their concerns. Once this perception gets set, it takes a lot of behavior—no amount of words will do—to change it.

To the more suspicious the advocate might be viewed as a patsy. This kind of response can quickly put the advocate on the defensive, which does not help. The advocate must realize and accept the fact that there are some segments of the community that have been so disserved by public bureaucracies that they will force into the open the matter of loyalty. You cannot serve two masters; you cannot represent my interest or my child's interest while serving the system's interest; you cannot get services accountable to "us" when you are accountable to "them." This either-or, us-them loyalty boundary is so deep and so high and so wide that the advocate cannot go over, under, or around it. It must be acknowledged and it must be admitted as one of the barriers to be overcome. It cannot be talked away, argued away, or persuaded away. It will be with you for a time. What you do and the way you do it, your style, over time will be the only evidence that will make any real difference on this point.

The very situation described above is itself a trap. The trap is the temptation to identify with the aggressor and to set out to prove your counter-bureaucracy motivation, or to assure "them" that you are above the bureaucracy. This is usually not productive for anyone, but especially is it unproductive for the advocacy process. As an advocate one must work with the systems that contain the resources. Those systems are frequently encumbered by bureaucracy beyond anyone's wish or desire. To help in the process of disencumbering the bureaucracy of unnecessary constraints or de-bureaucratizing superfluous bureaucratic service systems, the advocate does not go in swinging and proceed to clobber bureaucrats wherever he finds them.

Again the principle obtains: if I am to help I must first understand;

in order to understand I must try to look from the inside out. In order for the advocacy process to be fully engaged and workable, lines of communication must go deep into the bureaucracy. Bureaucratic alliances are essential for a within-system approach. It is not a question of whether advocates will work with bureaucrats. It is rather a question of how that work can best be accomplished such that the advocacy process functions without compromising the credibility of either the advocate or the bureaucrat. That is very difficult.

Somewhere between the extremes of becoming, or being viewed as, a patsy of the bureaucracy by members of the community on the one hand, or bureaucratic enemy number one by the bureaucrats on the other, there are miles of diplomatic space for the advocate's work. There are, indeed, times when the advocate must choose to oppose the bureaucracy. At other times he must choose to support it. And there are times he elects to rise above it. His choices must be honest and carefully considered, and his reasons must be made known. Reasons for decisions like this need to be oriented to specific issues that can be communicated and understood. A political rationale for this kind of decision is rarely acceptable to anybody. The advocate has his niche and his identity well established when bureaucrats and private citizens alike can anticipate and reasonably well predict where he will stand. Until that, time, however, this is the hill on which crosses are erected.

The Importance of Credibility with the Public

The importance of public credibility may not be fully appreciated until it is jeopardized or needed when it is not present. This is the ultimate authority base for the advocate. There are no short cuts to it and there are no substitutes for it. Without it advocacy cannot survive. Without it advocacy should not survive.

Credibility is the one thing over which the advocate has exclusive rule. No one else controls it, no one else can take it from him, and no one else can grant it. It is earned or lost in his behavior. His credentials may encourage certain initial assumptions but his credibility will ultimately rest on his interactions in and with the community. Credibility is logically discussed as an aspect of style. It could, however, be reversed with style's being discussed as an aspect of credibility.

The advocate needs to promote an air of openness, honesty, and integrity, for that is what he seeks in the system with which he works. He cannot promote openness unless he is open; he cannot require or even expect honesty unless he is honest. Most judgments of political naivete by which a lot of dishonesty is legitimatized are ill-founded.

The advocate needs to actively pursue and promote confidence. Trust and confidence are not the same as popularity. In some instances they are the deadliest of enemies. The confidence-building in which the advocate actively participates must be credible advocacy action.

In some quarters the advocate must accept the fact that he is guilty until he is proven innocent. He must also accept the fact that with some he will be accepted only to the extent that he is viewed as benign. Confidence comes hard and over time. It must be earned and deserved and it must begin with the advocate's own attitude and behavior.

Working without Walls

Organizations over time grow roots and develop shade, seeking stability and security. Organizations typically become larger and more complex. As this occurs, bureaucracy in the organization is increased and efficiency is reduced. As human-service agencies, for example, become larger and more bureaucratic, the energy and resources required for survival are increased.

As indicated earlier, it is not the purpose of this chapter to comment on the relative merits of bureaucracy *per se*. It is relevant, however, to note that bureaucracies do have certain characteristics and do develop organizational forms which provide, among other things, a certain amount of protection for those who work in them. Two basic points need to be made: (1) advocates do not and should not have the protection of bureaucratic insulation, and (2) advocacy programs should resist the natural drift of their own organization's becoming a bureaucracy. This has at least two major implications. First, the advocate must develop a style and some level of comfort in living in the open and without conventional organizational walls, bureaucracy. Second, advocacy programs should probably be kept small so that their own bureaucracy image and functions can be minimized.

The list of specific examples of bureaucratic impact on organizations could be quite long. Only four will be suggested here. Each represents organizational and system characteristics to which the advocate must relate in doing his or her work. Each also represents areas to be avoided, where possible, in advocacy systems.

RED TAPE

Very elaborate procedures, extensive forms, organizational lines, and waiting periods are a part of what those who become frustrated in trying to assess an organization refer to as "red tape." It makes sense as it is developed and put into place, usually one piece at a time, each piece having its own reason for being there at that time. There are many more "development" functions in organizations that result in the addition of new bureaucratic pieces, than there are housecleaning functions which reduce the unnecessary bureaucratic debris. The net results of adding procedure onto procedure and form onto form is a loss in efficiency and a gain in red tape.

There are other consequences. For instance: no individual has to defend or make sense out of the total system; no individual is forced to take consequential action; and individual members can separate themselves from service functions altogether. All of these are inconsistent with both the mission of advocacy and the spirit of advocacy.

There are two areas in particular that must be watched carefully. First, as has been stated earlier, records are important and uniquely so for the advocate in terms of accountability. But records can become a burden and no more than elaborated, nonfunctional, cabinet-filling files. The advocate cannot afford to begin to hide behind his or her own record system.

The other area to watch carefully is the process of modeling as the advocacy project interacts with bureaucracy. Legitimacy is in the work the advocate accomplishes, not in the organizational form developed. Organization is, of course, necessary. The motivation for organization, however, must be functional and not just to conform.

JARGON

Bureaucracies talk. They have their own language. The more they talk and the bigger they become, the more they talk to themselves. Acronyms, abbreviations, and numbers increase the bureaucracies' separateness and decrease the ability of "outsiders" to penetrate. The language of professional disciplines, supported by professional guilds, is sometimes incorporated into the language of the organization. This is particularly true in human-service bureaucracies. This contributes to the mystique, and to some extent the mystery.

Language is very important. The point here is that it can be used to communicate or it can be used to mystify. The language of labels and categories for disability or deviant populations is an example of the abuse of language in a bureaucracy. The social consequences for labeling a child mentally retarded, for example, are enormous.

Advocacy may have a language problem at the very outset in the use of the word *advocacy*. If that is the case then the word should be abandoned and a better word to communicate the social mission developed. Advocacy must be careful with its definitions as well as with its words. It must seek to communicate and open up, not to mystify and keep away. The protective function of jargon is inappropriate for advocacy and would ultimately be defeating.

BEHIND THE DESK

The architecture and organization of space in the bureaucracies are full of messages and meaning. One example is the use of the desk to separate oneself from whatever is on the other side. Another is the use of the office that serves several functions. This office declares very clearly the matter of ownership or territory: "You are in my office"; "I control the door." It also sets the officer away from the rest of the world.

People in organizations usually have offices. Offices have furniture, and so forth. If the advocate spends most of his time in an office and behind a desk, he is effectively unavailable to many of the people. He stands apart from many.

The advocate needs to identify as much as possible with the people whom he is advocating. He needs to pay careful attention to the space he occupies relative to his work and what that space means to the people.

RULES AND DECORUM

The advocate must abide by the rules that facilitate his work. These are usually developed over time with his constituency and through any mechanisms that may have needed to be developed to support his work. The advocacy project must be careful and very deliberate in the development of policy so that policies are facilitative and not inhibiting.

In large bureaucracies there is frequently a rule for everything. There is also commonly a general practice of understood and acceptable rule-breaking. This is a result of the discontinuity in the process between people who establish rules and those who abide by them. This does not contribute to a good working environment.

Bureaucratic ritual is important: "Things are done this way here." Ritual is not bad. In fact, it can be a very positive aspect of the organizational character. But there are different kinds of ritual. For example, some ritual is a matter of organization habit, commonly known as routine. This is good for efficiency so long as it does not become organizational rigidity and inhibit the ability of the organization to change and be responsive to legitimate needs and requests. There are many other kinds of rituals such as the ritual of celebration or of mourning. It would not be productive to pursue a detailed discussion of ritual forms here. It is sufficient to point out that the decorum and ritual of an organization can be positive features of the organization, helping it to accomplish its real mission, or they can be destructive features, detracting from its real mission. Advocacy must monitor its own ritualistic behavior.

Index

163

CHILD ADVOCACY WITHIN THE SYSTEM

was composed in 10-point Linotype Times Roman, leaded two points,
with display type in Ludlow Times Roman by Joe Mann Associates, Inc.;
printed on Hammermill 55-lb. Lock Haven by Wickersham Printing Co., Inc.;
Smyth-sewn and bound over boards in Columbia Bayside Linen
by Vail-Ballou Press, Inc.;
and published by

SYRACUSE UNIVERSITY PRESS

SYRACUSE, NEW YORK